VALUES, INC.

HOW INCORPORATING VALUES INTO BUSINESS AND
LIFE CAN CHANGE THE WORLD

Dina Dwyer-Owens
with Jordan Ochel

VALUES, INC.
How Incorporating Values into Business and Life Can Change the World

FIRST EDITION
Copyright © 2015 The Dwyer Group, Inc.,
and Dina Dwyer-Owens

Published by Beacon Publishing

ISBN 978-1-942611-05-9

Designed by Shawna Navaro and Leah Nienas

Printed in the United States of America.

TABLE OF CONTENTS

RESPECT

INTEGRITY

CUSTOMER FOCUS

HAVING FUN

ACTION

To my father for teaching me to incorporate
values at work
(Don Dwyer 1934 – 1994)

To my mother for grounding me in my faith

To my family at home and at The Dwyer Group for
allowing me to serve them as we strive to Live R.I.C.H.

and

To my husband, Mike and children, Dani and Mikey for
allowing me to do what I do

Foreword

This wonderful book is full of uplifting, inspiring stories and examples that make you want to be a better person.

Over the years, I have consulted and trained the executives and staff of more than 1,000 companies and organizations in 68 countries, working personally with more than five million people – at all levels.

In addition, I have conducted a series of Strategic Planning sessions for million-dollar corporations, each aimed at clarifying the Values, Vision, Mission, Purpose, and Goals of these organizations.

It has been said that there may be a better way to live than by practicing The Golden Rule ("Do unto others as you would have them do unto you"), but no one has yet found it.

In this book, and in all my work with top companies and individuals, the practice of The Golden Rule, and values, come first – especially the values espoused in this book.

There is a good reason for the central importance of values in human and business life: We all live from the inside out. Our outer worlds of performance and results tend to be mirror image reflections of our inner worlds' values and beliefs.

When you practice the principles taught in *Values, Inc.*, your outer life of rewards and satisfaction will follow naturally, like the day follows the night.

Above the temple of the Delphic Oracle in Greece are the words, "Man, know thy self."

One of the qualities of leaders at all levels and at each stage of their careers is that they know who they are, their true values, and they do not compromise them for any reason.

As Peter Drucker said, "Leaders are clear about their values, about the differences between right and wrong. They know what they stand for and they know what they will not stand for."

When you are clear about your values, and their order of importance, it is easier to make decisions and choose between alternatives.

When you live by your values and your innermost convictions, you experience feelings of self-esteem and personal value. Your self-image improves. Your self-confidence increases.

In our fast-moving world today, your values serve as an anchor – a foundation upon which you can build a wonderful life, characterized by self-respect and personal pride.

In reading this book, you are embarking upon a grand adventure into becoming the best person you could possibly be, and toward realizing your full potential for greater success and happiness.

Brian Tracy

Prologue

We must know that we have been created for greater things, not just to be a number in the world, not just to go for diplomas and degrees, this work and that work. We have been created in order to love and to be loved.
- Mother Teresa

It was January 2012, the prime-time hour. Months earlier, I had filmed an episode of the CBS Emmy Award–winning reality series *Undercover Boss*, and it was now on screens inside millions of homes.

Shortly after the episode ended, I was bombarded with e-mails, phone calls, web inquiries, cards, letters, tweets, Facebook mentions, and more. The viewers wasted no time letting me know that they were moved and inspired by the culture of our company, The Dwyer Group. Their comments were thoughtful and came from people of all walks of life—mothers, students, business leaders, prisoners, and AIDS patients. Their words and stories touched my heart and forever changed my life:

"Your company has renewed my faith in corporate America."

"Thank you for being so transparent and allowing yourself to be vulnerable and genuine."

"It's not often that you get to see a company operate with values and ethics."

"Thanks for renewing my hope in humanity."

How is it that a forty-five-minute reality show can renew someone's hope in humanity? Perhaps it was the love in action during the episode that did it for some of the viewers.

Wait. Love? At a company?

Yes. Love. It's the purpose of life, and there should always be room for love wherever you are, including at work. At The Dwyer Group, we call it "Living R.I.C.H."—living purposefully with respect, integrity, customer focus, and having fun in the process. The Dwyer Group is by no means a perfect company, and we would never claim to be. After all, if every organization is run by human beings, why would ours be an exception?

But values aren't just for companies; they're for you and me, friends and family, parents, children, old and young alike. Values are for all of us. So even though this book primarily centers its examples around the corporate setting, these values all begin at home.

When you express values such as respect and integrity in your words and deeds, you send the message to others that they are worthy of receiving your expression of those values. In other words, they are valuable. And what's a higher expression of love than that?

No matter who you are or what you do, or how old or young you are, know that you are not just a number in this world and that this book is written with you in mind.

Dina Dwyer-Owens

Chapter 1

Where It Begins

Your actions speak so loudly that I cannot hear what you say.

- Ralph Waldo Emerson

Ben leans in and says in a hushed voice, "I once overheard him saying his favorite vacations are excursions so dangerous that someone could die." He rises back up, smirking.

"Really?" Lisa says. "The CEO actually said that?"

Ben nods slowly, biting his lip. "Anyway, read this and come by my desk to sign an acknowledgment form before the end of the day." He drops a small booklet on her desk before walking away, disappearing into the vast field of workstations.

Lisa turns back to face her new workstation, a bay of three monitors on her horizon. She picks up the booklet, "Code of Ethics." She flips through several pages, finally settling on the section with the subheading "Values." She begins to read.

Respect
We treat others as we would like to be treated ourselves. We do not tolerate abusive or disrespectful treatment. Ruthlessness, callousness, and arrogance do not belong here.

Integrity
We work with customers and prospects openly, honestly, and sincerely. When we say we will do something, we will do it; when we say we cannot do something, then we won't do it.

Communication

We have an obligation to communicate. Here, we take the time to talk with one another . . . and to listen. We believe that information is meant to move and that information moves people.

Excellence

We are satisfied with nothing less than the very best in everything we do. We will continue to raise the bar for everyone. The great fun here will be for all of us to discover just how good we really can be.

Wow, she thinks, *this is great! I've never seen a company this serious about values.*

"Hey, I'm Dave. You're new here, right?" She turns toward the voice behind her. A stout man holds out his hand. She shakes it.

"Yeah, it's my first day."

"Cool. Well, don't let that stuff psych you out," he says, pointing to the page she was just reading. "The only part they really take seriously is Excellence. Have you heard about the performance reviews here?"

Lisa shakes her head.

He snorts. "It's called 'Rank and Yank.' It's not just your boss that reviews you; your teammates rate you as well. You're rated on a scale from one to five with one being the top performers. Each department is required to fire fifteen percent of all the fives on the team every year, even if they're decent employees. It's pretty brutal, actually. But I was a one my first year and got a five-million-dollar bonus. Not a bad gig for the winners, huh?"

He watches her expression, looking for a sign of approval. After a moment of silence, he continues, "Anyway, there's only one thing we all want here: money. All the executives openly admit that's their biggest goal too. If you're willing to do anything, you can get filthy rich in this place. So, a word to the wise: Watch your back—there's no such thing as friends here. It's every man for himself." Dave walks away.

That was strange, she thinks.

After Lisa finishes reading the booklet, she sets out to find Ben, her supervisor. When she finds his office, he notices her approaching his desk. "Did you finish it? Boring stuff, right?" He chuckles. "Here's the acknowledgment form." He slides it across his desk. "Sign this, work hard to impress us, and you'll get everything you ever dreamed of. Trust me, this company is going places."

He holds out a pen and smiles.

"Welcome to Enron."

Although the characters and dialogue in that story are fictional, the facts are not. The company's Code of Ethics, the aggressive performance reviews with mandatory 15 percent firings, the widespread and unabashed lust for money, the life-endangering adventures—all of them are true. It was CEO Jeffrey Skilling, in fact, who said that life-endangering adventures were his favorite. It was also Skilling who implemented the forced ranking evaluations at Enron.

To hear these things wouldn't be a surprise for anyone who knew his character. At Harvard Business School, he was a successful and driven student who was once asked by a professor what he would do if his company produced a product that might cause harm or death to his customers. He replied, "I'd keep making and selling the product. My job as a businessman is to be a profit center and to maximize return to shareholders. It is the government's job to step in if a product is dangerous."

In one act of corruption, there was no attempt by the executives to conceal their greed. After it was discovered by internal auditors that a top-performing oil trader at Enron had secretly funneled $2 million into a personal account, instead of being fired or even reprimanded, the thieving employee was praised by an executive for misdirecting external auditors and was told to "keep making us millions."

Today, it is apparent to everyone that the executives were never serious about their Code of Ethics. There were signs of the company's blatant disregard for ethical behavior everywhere. In fact, Enron's board voted twice to suspend the Code of Ethics when doing the legal and right thing stood in the way of large personal and company gains.

How could they not have seen the writing on the wall? What if they had been serious about their Code of Ethics? Would they have avoided one of the largest corporate bankruptcies and white-collar scandals in history?

At least one former Enron executive claims they would have. Andrew Fastow, former CFO, now admits, "I lost my moral compass and I did many things I regret." How many companies and executives over the past decades have we seen venture down the path toward the same sad fate?

Without a doubt, I truly believe living out shared values is one of the key factors to a company's lasting success. Thousands of successful companies around the world have a "code of ethics" or a "code of values" that has been embedded deeply in their culture. These codes are very similar to The Dwyer Group's Code of Values®. But unless a company's leadership exemplifies values in action, a boilerplate set of written values or ethics doesn't contribute to or define that company's success.

The Values, Inc. Compass

Why did I title the book *Values, Inc.*? Our values define us. They are the signposts we've chosen for our lives, reminding us of the direction we want to go. Sometimes we follow our values; too often we ignore them. *Inc.*, as you probably already know, is a business abbreviation that stands for "incorporated." If we *incorporate* our values into not only our business lives but also our personal lives, we will have a compass that shows us the direction toward personal and professional success, that shows us the journey to happiness and gives us the ability to change our lives and the lives of those around us. Many times, our compass comes from a person who changed our life, someone we aspire to be like, someone whose values we share.

My compass was given to me by my father, Don Dwyer.

To many, Don was a man of great respect and integrity. As a child of the Great Depression, he was driven by a vision of success. When he earned the right to lead half of a carpet-cleaning franchise in 1981, he didn't pick the highest-earning franchisees; he picked the most honest and ethical franchisees. For him, a person's success wasn't defined by money; it was defined by character and values. He knew that in order to build a company that could create positive change in the world, he first needed people who shared his vision and values.

He once said, "The strength of a business's foundation depends entirely on the values of the owner and of the people who operate the business." He knew you couldn't succeed in business or in life if you lowered your standards. To him, no amount of money or material things was worth putting the business at risk. So, how would he ensure that his vision of building a lasting, respectful company would outlive him? It began with the Code of Values he wrote and established within his first franchise company, Rainbow International Carpet Dyeing and Cleaning Company (today known as Rainbow International Restoration).

Don always said that his proudest accomplishment was when so many hardworking franchisees thanked him for helping them achieve their dreams. This was part of what made him an icon in the franchising industry. Changing people's lives and helping them achieve their dreams changed his life and helped him achieve his dreams too. I believe that changing lives is the first step toward changing the world, and it all begins with values.

This story of success through values is not unique to The Dwyer Group, however. Others include Southwest Airlines, JetBlue, Zappos, Disney, and Starbucks, just to name a few. These companies have reputations that instill trust in millions of customers. These brands stand in stark contrast to names like Enron, Lehman Brothers, and WorldCom. And it's not hard to think of the reason why.

Companies That Change the Paradigm

On Valentine's Day 2007, a JetBlue flight bound for Cancun, Mexico, was trapped on the tarmac for more than ten hours. The passengers were locked in a plane with no power, no food, inadequate lavatories, and no explanation for the delay. What made the whole ordeal even more infuriating was that the entire time, the terminal was in sight.

When the media picked up the news about the stranded passengers, the public response was a furor. Unlike many companies that would have put their public relations team into frenetic overdrive, JetBlue did not rationalize or excuse its behavior. Instead, the company openly admitted its mistake and apologized for the inexcusable delay.

But the people at JetBlue didn't stop there. They immediately got to work on creating a "Customer Bill of Rights" to ensure the company held itself accountable for any future delays or unforeseeable inconveniences by giving customers vouchers for future travel.

That wasn't the only time JetBlue's character was revealed to its customers. In the company's beginning months, there was a passenger suffering from diabetic shock. The plane had to be diverted for an emergency landing in order to get medical care to the passenger as quickly as possible. Realizing that the diabetic customer wasn't the only customer on the flight, founding member and current president and CEO, David Barger, stood outside the plane and personally apologized to each customer, giving each of them his phone number so they could book a free flight anytime in the future.

JetBlue also focuses on its internal customers (employees). In 2008, when the cost of jet fuel began to cripple the airline industry, Barger took a 50 percent pay cut so that the company could avoid laying off or cutting the pay of any employees. To help employees avoid future financial hardship, the company founded the JetBlue Crewmember Crisis Fund (JCCF), to which executives have donated more than $3 million to help crew members with financial troubles. This spirit of caring has caught on with the company's employees, who can contribute to the fund through an optional pay-period donation.

The company's values are so important that Barger accepts the responsibility, as president and CEO, of communicating them. He spends more than half of his time talking one-on-one with employees throughout the organization.

How many airlines extend the kind of respect and courtesy to their passengers and employees that JetBlue has repeatedly shown? More important, does it really take much more to change the paradigm than instilling strong values in a company and showing that you care with unexpected personal acts of kindness?

Leaders Who Change the Paradigm

At five a.m. in Hampton, New York, the ringing phone ends the nighttime silence. Howard answers. It's July 7, 1997, and he is told that several hours earlier three employees were shot and killed in a failed robbery attempt at a Starbucks in the Georgetown suburb of Washington, D.C. He immediately charters a flight to get there.

Upon arriving, Howard goes to the store to talk to the police. He puts out a $100,000 reward for information leading to the arrest of the murderer. After he gathers information about the employees who were killed, he visits the homes of the deceased employees to apologize to their grieving families and share their tears. He stays for a week, attends the funerals of the employees, and announces that future profits from the Georgetown store will be given as proceeds to a memorial fund to help local groups working to reduce violent crime and help victims.

Who is this man?

His name is Howard Schultz, and he is the CEO of Starbucks. Rather than immediately putting the company's public relations team to work, as most CEOs might be inclined to do, he booked the first flight to D.C. and spent a week doing everything he could to help the heartbroken community and families. He didn't decide that there was nothing he could do. Instead, he acted without hesitation and gave his time and heart to the families and the community.

"I was stunned. Catatonic," he says of first hearing the news. It's obvious by his actions that the event left an indelible mark on him. He even dedicated his first book to those three employees.

When CEOs like Howard Schultz and David Barger act genuinely, out of love and kindness, it seems to take people by surprise. It's sad that the unethical deeds of so many executives and politicians set the tone for what people have come to expect from their leaders. But when the tone is changed, it has powerful implications for society.

Why Values Are So Powerful

For the past several decades, the academic world has taken an active interest in the impact leaders have on companies. It turns out the impact is huge. Studies show that:

- 69 percent of American workers are dissatisfied with their ethical corporate climate

- An ethical corporate climate has a positive impact on employee retention and job satisfaction

- Job satisfaction, in turn, leads to organizational commitment

- An ethical corporate climate has a positive impact on the work engagement of employees

- Companies high in work engagement have nearly four times the growth in earnings per share (EPS) as companies in the same industry with low engagement

- Codes of ethics are crucial in influencing the ethical climate of companies and their employees

- When management sets the example of the code of ethics, it creates greater employee commitment than formal ethics training and leads to significant cost savings, improved performance, and increased profitability

- 73 percent believe that a code of ethics makes their company a better place to work

- 62 percent say that a code of ethics has helped change their behavior and direct their decisions

- 82 percent report that they often apply the code of ethics on the job

- Only 4 percent report that a code of ethics has no effect at all

- Companies with codes of ethics have above-average financial performance compared to those without codes

The value of values and their sweeping implications is hard to ignore. If we remember how much of a negative impact the past two decades of corporate scandals have had on the lives of millions of people, isn't it conceivable that if many of us implemented good values in our lives it could have an even greater positive impact?

Where Do Values Begin?

Values aren't just for the workplace. We all pick up values from our experiences and interactions with other people throughout our lives. In a survey of business professionals, 68 percent reported that the values they learned at home had the biggest influence on them. It's clear that how we raise our families has a far-reaching impact not just at home, but outside the home as well.

However, not all values are worthy or lasting. You may know people among your friends or family who live their lives in the sole pursuit of money, power, or fame. Their vision seems constantly clouded with material dreams, and they seem to devote much of their time and energy to these ends. They seem to value the material more than the intangible. Do these people seem less fulfilled, less happy, or less at peace to you?

Or maybe you are one of those people who have their values calibrated with money, power, or fame. If you look at your life and feel a need to change your values, it's not too late. It's never too late for happiness.

No matter who you are, you're a part of an increasingly distracted and rushed world. Globalization and the rise of the Internet Age have allowed humans to connect with more of what's *out there* in the world. The trouble with this is that we've forgotten to pay attention to what's *right here*. We've become more exposed to other people's values and allowed them to shift our own. We take part in other people's dreams and begin to believe that ours aren't big enough. People have become utterly absorbed in this new way of living. In the process, time has become a scarce commodity. These things have contributed to a decline in our connection with others.

Whether in the workplace or at home, we all set the tone. When the tone becomes negative or self-centered, it changes us and how we think and feel. Many of us see the effects of this in the world today and know it's time for change. Sadly, most people feel the problem is too large and think that change takes too much time and effort. But as Hyrum Smith says, "When people say, 'I don't have time,' what they're really saying is 'I value something else more.'"

If you find yourself saying, "I don't have time," what is it that is more important than taking part in a realignment of personal and cultural values? Our friends, our families, our workplaces, our society, and our happiness depend on it. Are the things you've been making time for really more important than these things? This is precisely the reason my father asked his family to hold ourselves to high ethical standards and to the pursuit of worthwhile endeavors.

Operating with a clear code of values is essential to building great organizations, thriving communities, loving families, and peaceful nations. When leaders focus on a set of values—especially written values—they establish signposts, daily reminders of how they strive to live their lives. These values are signposts for vision, strategies, and choices. They are guidelines for behavior and benchmarks for performance. But most people have not taken the time or even entertained the idea of having clear, written values by which to make their daily decisions. And most organizations that have taken the time to identify their values do not make the commitment to put them into action.

The Dwyer Group Code of Values®

Everyone's values can be stated in many ways, but the core aspects of the values held by ethical people are nearly all the same. In several studies carried out by the Institute for Global Ethics, respondents across multiple surveys collectively said that the four values most important to them are:

- Fairness

- Responsibility

- Respect

- Truth

Are those values important to you also? My guess is that you, like most people, would agree that they are. Do you treat your family with these values? If so, do you also use them at work? The Code of Values established at The Dwyer Group by Don Dwyer has guided the company toward success for more than thirty-three years. In 1994, at age sixty, my father passed away after suffering a massive heart attack. His death blindsided my family and was a huge blow to a company that had just gone public in 1993. But we wanted to ensure his legacy endured and that his spirit of values lived on within The Dwyer Group. What better way to do this than to reinvigorate the company with values defined by a new era of employees?

In 1996, we expanded the original Code of Values to a more clearly defined operational set of standards. The updated values would help us to more accurately define and measure the success of our company. After several months of collaboration, here is the Code of Values we follow to this day:

We live our Code of Values by. . .

Respect

. . .treating others as we would like to be treated

. . .listening with the intent to understand what is being said and acknowledging that what is said is important to the speaker

. . .responding in a timely fashion

. . .speaking calmly and respectfully, without profanity or sarcasm

. . .acknowledging everyone as right from their own perspective

Integrity

. . .making only agreements we are willing, able, and intend to keep

. . .communicating any potentially broken agreements at the first appropriate opportunity to all parties concerned

. . .looking to the system for correction and proposing all possible solutions if something is not working

. . .operating in a responsible manner, "above the line . . ."

. . .communicating honestly and with purpose

. . .asking clarifying questions if we disagree or do not understand

. . .never saying anything about anyone that we would not say to him or her

Customer Focus

. . .continuously striving to maximize internal and external customer loyalty

. . .making our best efforts to understand and appreciate the customer's needs in every situation

Having Fun in the Process!

Sometimes when I share our Code of Values with people who have never read them before, they ask me why it's so detailed and specific. I explain that it's better to set a high bar of values for our lives and meet them most of the time than to set a low bar and meet them all the time. When we define exactly what "respect" and "integrity" mean for us, we are on the same page and can share a common understanding of how we should interact.

This Code of Values has led our company to the success that we enjoy today; it is the foundation of the company. But more important than success, it has created a culture in which people aren't treated like *capital* or *resources*; people are *people*. Although this specific Code of Values is unique to The Dwyer Group, the words aren't what have contributed to our success, it's the basic values behind them—values shared in common with most people.

When most of us spend the majority of our lives at work, shouldn't we spend our time with those who treat us like a second family? Shouldn't there be mutual respect and integrity among teams who strive toward internal and external customer loyalty? *Shouldn't there be an atmosphere of fun? Shouldn't there be room for love?*

Ultimately, we gain these things through the expression of these values in our actions and words. This holds true for anyplace relationships are a focal point—work, school, church, or, most important, with friends and family.

Because our Code of Values has been so successful for our company, the following chapters of the book are individually centered around each of the values. But how do we *apply* our values to our personal and professional life? It all begins with authentic leadership.

Leading with Values

Leaders are everywhere. Leaders are your mother, your father, your teacher, your boss. They are your pastor and your hero; they are your friends and your family. Yes, even your enemies are leaders.

Leaders are defined as people who have an influence on the lives of others. This includes you; you are a leader. You have an influence on someone, whether you are a CEO or an intern, someone's parent or someone's child. In one way or another you lead *with your actions*. More often than not, a person's actions say a lot about whether or not his or her compass is calibrated by values. Good leaders lead with values in action; bad leaders lead with values missing in action.

What direction will you lead?

Respect

Every man is to be respected as an absolute end in himself, and it is a crime against the dignity that belongs to him as a human being to use him as a mere means for some external purpose.

- Immanuel Kant

Chapter Two

The Golden Rule Begins with Trust

We believe that people are basically good, we believe that everyone has something to offer, we believe that an honest, open environment can bring out the best in people, we recognize everyone as an individual, we encourage you to treat others the way you want to be treated.

- Pierre Omidyar, founder, eBay

There is a white house on the corner, humble in both size and appearance, weathered by the memories of more youthful days. The front door opens to a cool February afternoon, revealing an elderly woman framed by the dark interior. Her modesty is loosely veiled by a patterned dress suspended on one shoulder. The garment is a remnant of a time when independence didn't mean isolation, when it didn't mean the sudden onset of exhaustion from the day's necessary chores.

The hem of the woman's dress sways as she shuffles across the short lawn past the forgotten potted plants, past the sun-bleached plastic snowman. She holds in her hand a bag of trash that took her some effort to collect. As she approaches the curb, the remaining strength in her legs gives out. The moment lurches toward chaos as she tilts forward, her hands locked outward to brace herself on the pavement. The shock of hitting solid ground ripples through her. She cries out in pain and lies there, defeated. The breeze whispers across the trash bag beside her.

When she regains her will, she pushes herself upright. And there she sits, knees pointed up high above the ground, arms wrapped around her legs. The world around her continues on. To her right there is a large parking lot with too many cars. Walking toward a building is a trio of sharply dressed people, one of them laughing. A man passes them, walking in the direction of her house. As he gets closer he keeps his attention on her. He is finally close enough to ask her if she's okay. She swallows. "Well," she says, proceeding to explain what happened. She isn't injured, she says, but she can't stand back up.

He stands behind her and, with an arm wrapped around her, begins to lift her up to her feet. With care, he directs her toward the house, walking slowly. Her dress keeps slipping off her shoulder. Every time, he places it back on her shoulder to help her hold on to her modesty.

When they get inside, he helps her sit back in her chair. "I—I have money, over there, in that jar." She points unsteadily at it. "Take some. Let me tip you. Please." He politely refuses with a smile, even after she attempts multiple times to offer him recompense.

She welcomes his company and talks to him at length about random things, anything within her grasp to keep his interest, to keep his company and kindness. The tone in her voice is desperate, full of sadness. He sees this and, taking pity on her, listens, nods, smiles at the stories she strings together hastily just to hold on to the moment with him.

Eventually, the man asks if there is anything else he can do to help. After a long good-bye full of thank-yous and you're-welcomes and interjections, the man leaves. The elderly woman is relieved to be back inside and, long after the sun goes down, keeps replaying the day's events, touched by the unrelenting kindness this stranger showed her. She is amazed at how much a simple act of compassion, of love, can remind her that she is not alone and that she is still worthy of someone's time.

The man in this story is Patrick, and I'm proud to say that he works at our company, The Dwyer Group. He was walking from work toward his car when he came across the woman. Another associate saw the event and wrote about it in his nomination of Patrick for our bimonthly Live R.I.C.H. award. Needless to say, this story touched the hearts of everyone in our company and Patrick won the award. This act of kindness is the epitome of our first Code of Values: *We live our Code of Values by treating others as we would like to be treated.* This value, being at the top of our Code of Values, holds a position of significance. It is the Golden Rule, seen in nearly every culture and religion, and as this story shows, it is essential to the survival and growth of any society.

To act according to the Golden Rule requires empathy and love. To openly be treated according to the Golden Rule, especially by a stranger, requires trust. Trust requires you to take a leap of faith and believe that other people share the goodwill you hold in your heart. When the goodwill is affirmed, the trust is established.

The Beginnings of Relationships

Kindness and trust are the beginnings of any worthy relationship. Relationships built on these two things are too often left in the parking lot of any workplace, typically at workplaces where the mission of the company is focused solely on profits, the bottom line, and material possessions. This is unfortunate, because research shows that materialistic individuals are more competitive, tend to treat friends in objectifying ways, express less empathy, and tend to feel more alienated. This research goes against the words of Ivan Boesky, white-collar criminal, who once told students at the University of California, "Greed is all right, by the way. I want you to know that. I think greed is healthy. You can be greedy and still feel good about yourself."

If Ivan is right, imagine if Patrick were like this. Do you believe he would still stop and help the woman, much less spend as much time listening to her as he did? Would he feel good about himself if he ignored the woman? How easy would it be to trust him?

Whether or not an employee is materialistic isn't the only factor of his or her trustworthiness. In fact, studies show that employees' feelings about whether a company cares about their well-being impact the likelihood that they will cheat if they believe they can get away with it.

Trust in Society

To economists, researchers, and business professionals, the idea that trust plays a significant role in the well-being of our lives, businesses, and society comes as no surprise, especially after the economic scandals of the past several decades. Nobel Prize–winning economist Kenneth Arrow says that "it can be plausibly argued that much of the economic backwardness in the world can be explained by the lack of mutual confidence." Perhaps this is because, as Pulitzer Prize–winning journalist Thomas Friedman says, "without trust, there is no open society, because there are not enough police to patrol every opening in an open society. Without trust, there can also be no flat world, because it is trust that allows us to take down walls, remove barriers, and eliminate friction at the borders." He also says, "No low-trust society will ever produce sustained innovation." Marketing guru, Seth Godin, explains all of this in simpler terms. "In virtually every industry," he says, "the trusted brand is the most profitable."

We are all a part of a global society, one that is diverse and vast. With seven billion people on the planet, it is difficult to have the kind of small society like the townships so prevalent in our past. In these townships, everybody knew everybody else—who could be trusted and who couldn't. Small societies are all but impossible in the age of the Internet and the global economy. This is why trust is so important—since we can't reduce the size of society, we must earn the trust of others and, in so doing, raise the level of awareness about our perceived trustworthiness.

What makes all of this true? What is the correlation between a successful and sustainable business model and the level of trust in a society? Economists Paul Zak and Stephen Knack report, "High-trust societies produce more output than low-trust societies." This is because "trust reduces the cost of transactions."

Unfortunately, the way businesses advertise in today's world is so disjointed that it makes trust difficult. Commercials, billboards, and magazine inserts all stake the value of their ads on the claim that the business knows its customers, when in actuality the business may know nothing about or have nothing in common with its customers. Although marketing research has developed more sophisticated techniques throughout the years, this truth remains the same.

With so many esteemed leaders and researchers in society who know that trust is indispensable for a healthy society with sustained success, why are there still so many leaders, CEOs, and politicians who share Ivan Boesky's philosophy of greed?

Sensing the Motives of Leaders

Even before the 2008 crisis, there was a pervasive, ingrained sense of greed among business leaders and politicians, which led to crooked behaviors. It wasn't just the companies that made the news beat, either. A survey by KPMG in 2000 found that 76 percent of employees observed illegal or unethical conduct on the job that, if exposed, would seriously violate the public trust. In other words, the problem is more widespread than Enron or Lehman Brothers; those are just the companies that got caught. So the results of dozens of other surveys come as no surprise to us:

- Sixty-nine percent of Americans are dissatisfied with the ethical climate of society.

- Only 51 percent of employees have trust in senior management.

- Seventy-six percent have less trust in senior management than they did the previous year.

- Only 7 percent of employees believe that the values their leaders claim to have are consistent with their actions.

- Fifteen percent of employees feel that they work in a high-trust environment.

- Twenty-two percent believe business executives have "very high" or "high" honesty and ethical standards.

    - The same study reveals other professions with surprsingly higher percentages of honesty and ethical standards:

        - Bankers (27 percent)

        - Auto mechanics (29 percent)

        - Judges (45 percent)

    - Lawyers and TV reporters (both 20 percent) had only slightly lower perceptions of honesty and ethical standards.

- Only 25 percent of employees trust management to make good decisions in uncertain times.

- Only 10 percent feel their organization holds people accountable for results.

• Only 13 percent have cooperative working relationships with other departments.

• Twenty-nine percent of employees believe their management cares about their professional development.

• Only 42 percent believe their management cares about them in any way.

These findings aren't merely uncomfortable; they have a tangible and devastating impact on organizations and our society.

The Damage of Low Trust

The damage of a low-trust organization isn't in what the absence of trust causes, but rather in what it means the company lacks: the benefits of high-trust organizations. Trust leads to several advantages in a company, such as improved job performance, increased employee commitment, and more open communication, leading to improved problem solving. Other benefits include higher levels of cooperation and greater employee perception of fairness.

Already it is becoming clear just how much trust and the Golden Rule go hand in hand, and the relationships between employees and their management are no different. Because of the impact leaders have on our lives, their actions and, indeed, their very character transcend personal responsibility and approach a realm of greater responsibility. The level to which employees trust management is a significant factor in the success of a business. When that trust exists, employees are more willing to go beyond their job requirements to work in ways that benefit the company. It also leads to increased levels of courtesy, sportsmanship, conscientiousness, altruism, virtuosity, and satisfaction with both the job and leaders.

Leaders bred from a traditional, almost industrialist managerial philosophy might ask how trust can fit effectively into a purist, laissez-faire version of a capitalist economy. Former chairman of IBM John Akers gives a clear and powerful explanation of the important role trust actually plays in our economy:

Ethics and competitiveness are inseparable. We compete as a society. No society anywhere will compete very long or successfully with people stabbing each other in the back; with people trying to steal from each other; with everything requiring notarized confirmation because you can't trust the other fellow; with every little squabble ending in litigation; and with government writing reams of regulatory legislation, tying business hand and foot to keep it honest. That is a recipe not only for headaches in running a company, but for a nation to become wasteful, inefficient, and noncompetitive. There is no escaping this fact: the greater the measure of mutual trust and confidence in the ethics of a society, the greater its economic strength.

But despite Akers's wisdom, and despite the fact that today's society is more competitive than ever before, organizational problems still exist and leaders using traditional management models wonder why they lack the trust they expect from employees. On the other hand, when leaders treat employees as people, as valuable assets of the company, they are characterized as high trust individuals. Studies show that profitability is significantly higher in high-trust companies than in low-trust companies. One study showed that total shareholder returns were 286 percent higher in high-trust companies. Another, conducted over a thirteen-year period, showed that high-trust companies outperformed the market by 288 percent!

Voices of Reason, Voices of Change

When the evidence stares us down, daring us to change, will we listen? Or will we hold on to an outmoded philosophy that has a far-reaching negative impact, no matter how good our intentions may be? When we live in a society whose trust in leaders and companies is continually declining, something has got to give, and it starts with the leaders.

When leaders begin to put others first, they find that, rather than taking advantage of management, employees actually reciprocate over time. What if we all put each other first? Howard Gardner, a Harvard professor, says that a person with an ethical mind asks him- or herself, "What kind of a person, worker, and citizen do I want to be? If all workers in my profession adopted the mindset that I have and did what I do, what would the world be like?"

It is this kind of question that we need to ask ourselves daily; as social beings it is our responsibility toward one another. Without each other, values wouldn't exist. Henrik Høgh-Olesen, the head of psychology and behavioral sciences at Aarhus University, in Denmark, believes that human survival relies on finding ways to live together in peaceful and mutually beneficial ways. In other words, a single person living in a world by himself "needs no moral rules, as he has no one but himself to harm, offend, or treat unfairly." But the fact that we aren't alone and that we live in a society with other individuals, he argues, has created behaviors such as giving, trust, and respect.

The fact that we have values because we are social beings means that we share the impact that values have on our lives. As Warren Buffett puts it: "Trust is the air we breathe—when it's present, nobody really notices; when it's absent, everybody notices." So trust and love have this airlike quality in common. A change in our perspective can lead to the motivation to change our actions. A change in our actions can change the world. As one of my personal heroes, Mother Teresa, puts it, "Every act of love is a work of peace, no matter how small."

Patrick gave peace to a frail and lonely woman on a curbside. His love inspired him to show kindness she might not have thought could possibly come from a stranger. In this way, Patrick is an example of the selflessness and peace found in the Golden Rule. His actions contribute to the trustworthiness of The Dwyer Group. An increased trust in our company has a positive impact not only on profitability but also on the trust and kindness we, in turn, give back to society. One act is enough to change a heart. One heart is enough to change a mind. One mind is enough to change our perception of each other and ourselves.

E. E. Cummings, famous American poet, essayist, author, and playwright, said it best: "We do not believe in ourselves until someone reveals that deep inside us something is valuable, worth listening to, worthy of our trust, sacred to our touch. Once we believe in ourselves we can risk curiosity, wonder, spontaneous delight or any experience that reveals the human spirit."

For the woman who fell to the pavement as she carried out her trash, the day ended well, not only because she was uninjured from her fall, not only because she made it safely back inside before dark—her day ended well because she met a kind man, and that man *listened*.

Trust and the Golden Rule
Value Reflection

How often are you consciously aware, *in the moment*, of how you're treating someone else?

When was the last time a stranger treated you kindly? Harshly? What about a coworker or acquaintance? Whom would you trust?

Do you know anyone at school or work who is often ignored? Who is often difficult to work with? How can you do one nice thing for each of them *today*?

Reflect on how doing those nice things made you feel. Did the people react how you thought they would? *Does it matter how they reacted?*

Chapter Three

Listening Begins with Silence

We've all heard the criticism "he talks too much." When was the last time you heard someone criticized for listening too much?

- Norm Augustine, former chairman, Lockheed Martin

It's the day after Mother's Day and it's already like any other Monday morning. Ted gathers his invoices from his restoration and carpet-cleaning jobs from the day before. He walks into his boss's office.

"Morning, Mike. Here are my invoices." He sets the invoices on his boss's desk.

"Ah, thanks, Ted." Mike sets his coffee mug down and reaches for the stack of papers. "Hey, there's doughnuts in the break room, by the way."

"Thanks, boss!" Ted smiles. He leaves and walks into the break room. After pouring a cup of coffee into a small Styrofoam cup, he lifts the flimsy cardboard lid of a box on the table. He hooks a doughnut and takes a bite.

"Ted, can you come into my office for a minute, please?" Mike is standing in the doorway with a serious expression on his face. He turns around and heads back toward his office.

Ted swallows slowly and walks to Mike's office. Mike pokes at an invoice on the desk and says, "Please explain this." Ted walks over and picks it up. At the bottom of the itemized invoice he reads what he wrote the day before: *Scotchgard. No charge.*

"Well, I just decided to Scotchgard the carpet in this lady's house for free."

Mike looks frozen in surprise. He scoffs, "Her *whole* house?"

"Yes, sir. I can explain."

"That's easy for you to do, Ted, because you're not the one who has to pay for it. An entire house worth of Scotchgard is a lot of product you've just given away for free!"

"I—I was just . . . Let me explain."

Mike's jaw clenches and he pinches the bridge of his nose, struggling to maintain composure. "I don't want to ever see this happen again. You're wasting our products."

"But, I—"

"You're dismissed, Ted, thank you."

Ted sighs and leaves quietly.

Work continues slowly, uncomfortable hours stretching out the day. The silence of the afternoon is rattled by an unexpected call. Mike answers.

"Thank you for calling Rainbow International. Mike speaking."

A lady responds tearfully, "I just want to tell you guys that your company is the only one I'm going to use from now on. Your guy came in and did such a great job. I just happened to mention in passing that my kids forgot to get me something for Mother's Day. He Scotchgarded my whole house and said to me, 'Happy Mother's Day.' I just couldn't believe it! I will never use anybody besides your company again. He didn't have to do what he did, but he just gave me one of the most exceptional gifts of all time."

Moved by her story, Mike thanks the woman for calling and waits for Ted to return from a restoration job. When Ted returns, Mike promptly calls him to his office.

"I feel like an idiot," he says after Ted walks in. "I got a call from your customer and she explained to me why you Scotchgarded her house. Even though I don't advocate giving products away, you really went the extra mile for her and that's exactly what we want to have happen."

Ted nods slightly.

"Thank you for what you did. I'm sorry; I should have let you talk and tell me why you did it. I should've listened."

This is a story one of our franchisees from our Rainbow International brand told me. It is the perfect example of our value, "Listening with the intent to understand what is being said and acknowledging that what is said is important to the speaker." Leaders often take their responsibilities and leadership seriously. Unfortunately, their sense of duty can be so strong that they sometimes forget to listen to those they lead. This can cause complications in the workplace.

The Listening Advantage

Studies show that when employees feel they are heard and that their opinions count for something it can have a significant impact on things like employee retention, productivity, and customer satisfaction. These things have been shown to create an average gain in productivity of six percent.

What makes listening so powerful? Lee Cockerell, former vice president of operations at Walt Disney World Resort, puts it simply:

> When everyone matters and everyone knows he or she matters, employees are happy to come to work, and they're eager to give you their energy, creativity, and loyalty. The result is predictable: more productivity and satisfaction; less absenteeism and turnover. On the other hand, when people don't feel included, they become apathetic and perform at less than their full capacity. To put it simply, all people want exactly what you

want. You want to be included, listened to, respected, and involved, don't you? You want to be asked your opinion and have it taken seriously. You want to feel valued. And you want to be known as an individual and treated as such.

Employees are people, not commodities. They contribute to a business and are involved in so many aspects of a business that leaders couldn't ever experience on their own.

Body language is the most important part of communication. Being able to actually see what someone is trying to say is just as, if not more, important to understanding what he or she is trying to communicate. In 2012, I went undercover on *Undercover Boss* to learn more about the challenges our frontline team members face. When I would listen to their stories, I began to realize how much I need to listen with my eyes, not only my ears. Their body language revealed more to me than just their words. This discovery had such a profound impact on me during my *Undercover Boss* experience and seems to be the recurring theme of the show.

For some people, the word *leader* conjures images of a dictator ruling over his "subjects." This is a demeaning metaphor—those being led aren't subjects; they're leaders in other areas who allow themselves to be led by someone else better suited to the task at hand. When leaders don't listen, they give in to a dictator mentality and people begin to feel viewed as subjects. When leaders listen first, they humble themselves as servants and people begin to feel like valued equals.

Dictator or Servant?

Servant leaders aren't just another fad in management theory; they're one of the most fundamental aspects of successful business-es. This statement is backed up by several studies on the subject. One study finds that some of the most important aspects of a servant leader are:

- Listening intently and receptively to others

- Having empathy for others and trying to understand them

- Being both aware and self-aware

- Having the power of persuasion; influencing others by convincing them, not coercing them

- Possessing a knack for conceptualizing and communicating ideas

- Seeing him- or herself as a steward; i.e., as an individual whose main job is to serve others

- Being firmly dedicated to the growth of every single employee

- Being committed to building community in the institutions where people work

In any organization, we all contribute to a common goal of organizational success. We all have an important role to play, and servant leaders recognize this. That's why this form of leadership is so powerful.

Work is not about fulfilling leaders' fantasies of being monarchs, as the term "chain of command" would suggest; it's about working toward happier, more fulfilling lives for all stakeholders, from the CEO to interns to customers. When this perspective doesn't guide the motives of leadership, organizations begin to break down. But when serving others, compassion, happiness, and respect become the guiding principles of everyone involved, which leads to organizations building a far stronger foundation for success.

Communication is a crucial aspect of business, of *life*. Larry King once said, "My first rule of conversation is this: I never learn a thing while I'm talking." Our survival depends on learning; learning depends on listening. If we can't trust those who don't want to learn, how can we trust those who don't listen?

Listening
Value Reflection

Can you name three people in your life who you feel truly listen to you? What qualities make them good listeners?

Can you name three *different* people in your life who you think would say that you truly listen to them? Why would they say that you are a good listener?

Are there any people in your life who you feel don't "get" you? If so, when you're talking with them, what is it about their behavior that makes you feel that way?

Can you recall, in detail, the last conversation you had with someone that lasted more than fifteen minutes? If not, why? What can you do to better remember the details of your next conversation?

Chapter Four

Timeliness

The cost of not doing anything or inaction is huge. We would rather do something and have an answer, even though it may not be the right one, instead of waiting and not doing anything.

- Meg Whitman, former president and CEO, eBay

Two minutes into US Airways flight 1549's ascent, a formation of geese approaches the airplane. The speed of the impact is over 250 miles per hour. The loud drone of the engines suddenly becomes background noise as the birds thump against the windshield like a burst of hail. In an instant the captain's view of the world outside the cockpit becomes blotches of dark brown. The engines go silent and the exhaust begins flaming. Fumes start to fill the cabin. "All passengers brace for impact," the captain announces. He radios air traffic controllers to let them know that at their rate of descent, they are unable to return to LaGuardia Airport. With the lives of 155 passengers at the mercy of his wit and composure, he prepares the airplane for landing in the Hudson River. Six minutes into the flight, all passengers are shaken but safe and preparing for ditching the plane.

It is for his quick thinking that Captain Chesley "Sully" Sullenberger became a national hero and a symbol of courage. The event became known as the "miracle on the Hudson" and is a testament to the significance of timely response to difficult situations.

With the level of impact that businesses have on people's lives, it becomes a basic responsibility of any company to respond quickly to its customers' needs. Why? In a world where breaking news vies for our attention and our social media feeds refresh every second, the cost of inaction rises with the rate of global connectivity. A study by Edison Research reveals that 32 percent of customers who reach out to a company on social media expect a response within thirty minutes. When the customer reaches out regarding customer support, 57 percent expect the company to offer the same response on nights and weekends as during normal business hours. Unfortunately, the average response time of businesses on Twitter is just over eleven hours. So, who's listening? After all, that's what a response is: an action prompted by listening. This is what customers expect.

The cost of untimely responses is one that most businesses neglect to think about. Thirty-eight percent of customers report having more negative feelings about a company when they didn't receive a timely response. But when the social media engagement between customer and company is positive, active, and timely, those customers spend 20 to 40 percent more money with that company. Although this book is not a treatise on social media, it does provide relevant information on the virtue of timeliness, which is this: When you listen and actively engage with your customers and your employees by responding to positive and negative interactions in a timely fashion, you show with your actions that you value them.

Sometimes, however, the cost of delayed response—especially when a company must own up to a larger mistake—can be more than millions or billions of dollars; it can cost lives.

In 2004, Laura Christian had one of the happiest days of her life when she reunited with the daughter she had given up for adoption at birth. A year later, she would experience one of the saddest days of her life.

It is July 29, 2005, in Southern Maryland. A sixteen-year-old girl could never know as she drives her Chevrolet Cobalt that this ride will be her last. She could never know that when her car collides with a tree in the dark, becoming a mass of shriveled metal wrapped around the tree, her airbags will not deploy. She could never know that the airbags will not deploy because of a faulty ignition switch. She could never know that this defect is one that General Motors has known about for more than three years but has remained silent about.

At five a.m., an hour after the crash, Laura Christian's phone rings. She answers to the somber voice of her daughter's adoptive mother telling her that their daughter is dead. Laura's screams disturb the morning hours. Her beautiful daydreams of a happy future with her daughter in her life have been stolen from her. The bright and joyful future her daughter dreamed for herself has been stolen from her. The culprit? A tiny spring designed 1.1 millimeters too short. This spring controls the electrical safety system in the car.

Nearly ten years and thirteen deaths later, on February 13, 2014, GM finally began the recall of more than 600,000 cars linked to this issue. And yet, the year before the girl's death, engineers at GM had developed a fix to the ignition switch issue, but executives at the company had turned the suggestion down due to the cost of the fix and the amount of time required to fix it. Two months before her death, another engineer had proposed an alternate fix but was rejected by executives as well. As of the date of this writing, the recall has been expanded to 8.5 million cars and GM has been fined $35 million. The cost of a single working ignition switch…

Ninety cents!

Although the majority of businesses don't face anything even remotely this costly or deadly, this is a magnified parable of the value of timeliness. What if General Motors had responded when engineers had spotted the issue and discovered a fix? What if ego and corner cutting hadn't clouded the judgment of the company's executives year after year? What if it hadn't taken the company more than a decade to finally admit the problem and their fault? What if, in the beginning, General Motors had responded in a timely fashion? There would still have been a recall, but it would not have been as expensive because there would have been fewer cars. There would be no $35 million fine. There would be no irreparable damage to the brand.

Thirteen people might not have lost their lives.

Timeliness
Value Reflection

Have you ever put off dealing with a difficult situation? Would it have been better if you'd dealt with it shortly after if happened?

Have you ever used traffic or alarm clock issues as a false excuse for being late to work, class, or a meeting? Why? How did it make you feel? What are some other false excuses you've used?

Think of a time when someone has repeatedly forgotten to return an item he or she borrowed from you. How did it make you feel? Why did it make you feel that way?

Chapter Five

Our Words

Keep your thoughts positive because your thoughts become your words. Keep your words positive because your words become your behavior. Keep your behavior positive because your behavior becomes your habit. Keep your habits positive because your habits become your values. Keep your values positive because your values become your destiny.

- Mahatma Gandhi

Four-letter words can set the tone of a conversation, or sometimes a relationship. When we think back on some of the most heated arguments in our lives, how many of them have included profanity? Some people have experienced profanity used against them as a weapon by someone who is aggressive or even domineering. It may have started in their childhood with a verbally abusive parent, or the abuse may come from a spouse or other family member. When a person is spoken to with hurtful words on a consistent and unrelenting basis, it can leave a scar on their heart that holds their darkest memories. All it takes to reopen the wound is to hear those words again, even if the person using them utters them casually.

Have you ever noticed how young children tend to parrot their parents' offhand phrases that include bad language? It's as if they instinctively know the power of these words before they understand their meaning and taboo. Profanity is language designed to elicit an emotional response or that is used in conjunction with emotion, which is why many people use it in communication involving a range of emotional intentions: anger, aggression, sadness, humor, elation. The power of these words is indisputable to many, especially those who experience it so often and so negatively.

Words in the Workplace

The nursing profession is a difficult one laden with the kinds of challenges and emotions many of us don't face on a daily basis. Not the least of these challenges is the verbal abuse most nurses experience. In a study of 213 American nurses, more than 96 percent report that they experience verbal abuse:

- 79 percent from patients

- 75 percent from other nurses

- 74 percent from doctors

- 68 percent from patients' families

Imagine what kind of an impact this has on the mental and emotional lives of these nurses. Studies suggest that it increases stress levels; decreases morale; causes emotional fatigue; decreases productivity, retention, and recruitment; and negatively impacts the quality of health care. This shouldn't come as a surprise to anyone, especially as we read the words of a twenty-nine-year-old nurse in one study on the subject: "Here in Trauma, we are exposed to mostly verbal abuse, not really physical abuse. Most of the times it is just swearing . . . they are rude to you, they hurl all sorts of words at you . . . swearing at you and scolding you."

Hurling words. It sounds violent. It is violent. Her choice of phrase suggests that she was the target of weaponized words. And what can these words do but cause harm?

The Damage of Weaponized Words

Seventy-two percent of nurses in one survey agree that verbal abuse at nurses should not be tolerated. Despite this fact, a study of over forty-four hundred nurses in the United Kingdom shows that more than half of those who experience abuse do not report the incidents. This is due to their perception that it would not lead to changes in policy and the fear that they would fall under greater scrutiny or experience retaliation. Unfortunately, regardless of the high levels of psychological stress abused nurses experience, only 25 percent seek professional help. A nurse in one survey revealed that because of this stress, "they take all that home and . . . they have arguments with their kids or spouses and it is so unnecessary." The cycle of pain and stress continues outside the workplace, and it began with one tumbling, hurled word.

Perceptions in the Office

Many people argue that their use of bad language is harmless and not aggressive. While the majority of those who claim this are likely to be telling the truth in this regard, we have to ask ourselves why it seems to matter to so many people anyway. And it clearly does.

In 2012, CareerBuilder surveyed more than two thousand hiring managers and thirty-eight hundred office workers across many industries and company sizes. Although those surveyed are less likely to experience verbal abuse in their industries than those in the health care industry, their sentiments are similar. Here are some of the survey's findings:

- 51 percent of workers use bad language in the office

- 95 percent do so in front of coworkers

- 51 percent do so in the presence of their manager

- 13 percent do so in front of senior leadership

- 7 percent do so in front of clients

Employers have a lot to say on the subject as well:

- 64 percent said they would think less of an employee who used bad language repeatedly

- 81 percent said that abusive language calls an employee's level of professionalism into question

- Others say that employees who regularly use bad language exhibit lack of control (71 percent), immaturity (68 percent), and lower intelligence (54 percent)

- 57 percent said they would be less likely to promote employees who use abusive language in the workplace

So if the intent behind inappropriate language is harmless and not aggressive, why is it that workers are less likely to use such expressions in front of their boss's boss than in front of their peers? And why do employers perceive employees who use profanity less favorably?

The Power of Voice

The power of words is undeniable. Yet sometimes it's not just the words you choose, but your tone of voice. Sarcasm is a popular form of humor, especially in the United States. It shows, I think, a level of emotional intelligence to pick up on sarcasm intended as harmless banter. But sometimes the delivery of sarcasm can be lost in translation and have unintended consequences. Sometimes the consequences are intended. Sarcasm can be risky in the workplace and can have the same negative effects as any other form of verbal abuse.

In 2004, we acquired a company called Harmon AutoGlass—a company of more than twelve hundred employees—with the goal of making Glass Doctor the largest footprint of any auto glass company. I traveled across the country conducting town hall meetings in order to introduce The Dwyer Group to those new employees and help them understand what our transition plan was. During those meetings, I introduced our Code of Values and our system for "beeping" one another. I told the story of how, after we developed our Code of Values, the leadership of the company told all of the employees that over the next ninety days they should beep us whenever they caught us violating a value. When I told them how often we heard beeps around the office, the chuckles in the room began.

At the end of one of my presentations, I held a Q&A session. One of the employees at the back of the room raised his hand and asked me a question with a very sharp, sarcastic tone of voice. I responded in what I felt was a very firm and frank manner. Two people in the room beeped me within seconds. When I asked them why, they said it was because I was very sarcastic in the way I answered the question. I was floored to find out I had been sarcastic; I never thought of myself that way. And yet, it was clear to a roomful of people who had just met me that I was. Immediately, I apologized to the gentleman for being sarcastic. What happened next surprised me. He said, "No, I owe *you* an apology. I should never have asked the question in the tone of voice that I did." In that moment, we both took responsibility and were able to move forward without friction.

But it's not just sarcasm—being ignored, patronized, or yelled at are other ways that people can be hurt by someone's tone. As researcher Jonathan Wolff puts it, these behaviors illustrate "failures of common courtesy." He says that it is insulting to be treated in this way, to be treated "with less respect than one deserves." Too many environments in our lives—such as work, church, and school—fail to extend common courtesy and respect to our peers. The leaders in our lives and in our homes set the tone.

Leaders on Language

I recently read about a former CEO of a Fortune 100 company who has an infamously colorful vocabulary. Her recorded usage of the *F* word appears many times in the public sphere, and it is often used in a threatening or derogatory manner. It even got to the point where her employees asked her to tone down her language. Her *employees*. And yet she let it slip on a call with investors after promising her employees she would work on holding her tongue. There is no question that being the CEO of such a major public company is stressful, but exhibiting a lack of restraint leads to a lack of respect.

David Green, CEO and founder of Hobby Lobby, understands how important it is to pay attention to your speech. "I think people expect me, the CEO, to express myself in respectful terms." He says that the company doesn't have firm rules about this for its employees. However, it's clear that Hobby Lobby wants its employees to think carefully about how they choose their words. "[W]e have posted a sign at the various entrances to our warehouse that says the following: 'Language is the expression of thought. Every time you speak, your mind is on parade. Keep it clean.'"

"Don't underestimate the power of word choices," says Lee Cockerell, former vice president of operations at Walt Disney World. "So make sure your workplace vocabulary conveys the appreciation and respect you have for your employees." He's not just talking about profanity or sarcasm; he also advises leaders to find substitutes for unflattering and derogatory terms. For example, *as-*

sociate instead of *underling*, and *partner* instead of *inferior*. "Come up with language that captures the spirit of your organization. . . . Your employees will feel more respected, appreciated, and valued."

Right or Wrong?

Although I don't believe abusive language is necessary in any situation, this chapter isn't a debate about whether bad language, sarcasm, or pessimistic talk is right or wrong; it's about how it affects those around us, especially when the way it's used is intentionally hurtful and negative. It's also about how it could affect our business. Even if customers use bad language, many are repulsed by businesspeople they interact with who use it.

This chapter, I hope, also helps provoke thoughts about how the words of others affect you too. Mahatma Gandhi was aware that harsh, demeaning, and negative thoughts have a strong impact on our lives, hearts, and minds. He once said, "I will not let anyone walk through my mind with dirty feet."

Although I may not use profanity and believe this choice is the right one, you may believe differently. By considering the impact of our words and our actions on others, we are recognizing that the world does not revolve around us. In doing so, we are listening to the perspectives of others and earning their trust and respect in the process.

Our Words
Value Reflection

Can you think of a time recently when someone's profane or vulgar language made you blush? Why did it make you feel that way? Did you tell the person?

Has anyone you've known taken sarcasm too far? Did it hurt your feelings? Was the person aware that he or she had hurt you?

Has anyone ever told you that your language is inappropriate? Do you agree with this? If not, why? If so, what can you do to be more considerate about how your words affect people around you?

Chapter Six

Perspectives

You must look within for value, but must look beyond for perspective.

- Denis Waitley, author and motivational speaker

We live on a planet of human beings. As individuals we make up a collection of characteristics, traits, and beliefs. Our unique perspectives are the result of memories, upbringing, tragedies, joys, successes, failures, and the experiences of a life lived. A world of differences doesn't have to be divisive; it can and should be a thing of beauty, a spectrum of the amazing human spirit on display. A world of sameness is a world that doesn't allow for personal growth.

In order to embrace the beauty of diversity, we have to embrace the beauty of ourselves. This requires transparency and acceptance. When we are genuine with others about who we are, we invite others to do the same. We don't have to agree on everything—which would be impossible, since no two lives are alike—but we should try to find the heart and the origins behind the beliefs of others. If we are true to ourselves and expect others to do the same, it is important to acknowledge our fellow humans as right *from their own perspective.*

Some of the biggest companies have histories that have been shaped by the personal values of their founders or executives. It is clear from the cultural diversity of companies like Apple, IBM, Chick-fil-A, and Hobby Lobby that leaders' personal values are not all the same. What makes these companies so successful? Perhaps it is the fact that in a world of advertisements and catering to interests and desires of customers, any genuine expression that comes from a company's leadership feels like an invitation to transparency in a realm (business) so often hesitant about sharing flaws or vulnerabilities, for fear of losing profit. Perhaps it is because to be genuine is to be authentic, and authentic leadership is important to people who want their leaders to lead by example.

What is the makeup of an authentic leader? According to one group of researchers, authentic leaders value and exhibit openness, trust, and transparency. From the perspective of Claudia Peus, of the Technische Universität München, authentic leaders are guided by specific moral standards even when it goes against the views of other groups and organizational and societal pressures.

Across from Dan sits a reporter for the Baptist Press. Dan, the president and COO of Chick-fil-A, is being interviewed about the company's biblical values.

"Your company has garnered both criticism and support for its stance on biblical values. Does your company also support the traditional view of the family unit?" As the reporter eagerly awaits a reply, Dan thinks of how to respond to a subject surrounded by so many emotions and varying perspectives.

"Guilty as charged," he says. "We are very much supportive of the family—the biblical definition of the family unit." Dan cannot foresee that these words will soon launch one of the most contentious public debates of 2012. Protesters will line up outside Chick-fil-A restaurants. Supporters of the traditional marriage worldview will line up inside the restaurants. It is rare for customers to gain personal insight into the lives and worldviews of business leaders; it is precisely this rare transparency that will lead Chick-fil-A to a 12 percent increase in sales in 2012.

Shane Windmeyer is the founder and executive director of Campus Pride, a national organization for lesbian, gay, bisexual, and transgender (LGBT) and ally college students. He is also a gay man who has been married to his husband, Tommy, for more than nineteen years.

Shortly after Dan's comments, Campus Pride began organizing protests against Chick-fil-A because of the company's donations to pro–traditional marriage organizations. Later in the year, an incident deeply affected Shane and the entire LGBT community.

On a college campus, one fraternity gathered in the campus Chick-fil-A restaurant. Anytime an openly gay student would walk by, the fraternity would shout, "We love Chick-fil-A," followed by a series of gay slurs.

When Dan hears about the incident on the college campus, he is concerned about the students who were affected by it. After a time, he is able to track down the phone number for the founder and executive director of Campus Pride through a mutual business friend. "His name is Shane," the friend says.

Dan dials the number on his cell phone. The line rings.

Shane answers. "Hello?"

"Hi, Shane. This is Dan Cathy. How are you?"

Shane hesitates for a moment. *Is he going to give me a piece of his mind?* "I'm—I'm good, thanks. And you?"

Much to Shane's surprise, Dan begins a conversation that lasts an hour. He asks Shane questions about Campus Pride and the LGBT community in the spirit of gaining a deeper understanding, a civil and peaceful understanding.

Over the next several weeks, Dan and Shane continue a series of phone conversations and text messages, which eventually leads to in-person meetings.

Dan walks in and smiles widely at his new friend. He holds out his hand. "It's good to finally meet you, Shane." Shane extends his hand and returns Dan's smile.

After sitting through several dialogues, Shane learns of an internal document called "Who We Are." In it is a statement regarding the company's value of treating "every person with honor, dignity, and respect."

Dan thanks Shane for allowing him into his life. Although he can't merge Shane's lifestyle with his religious beliefs, he respects Shane's perspective. Dan explains to Shane, "This is the blessing of growth."

After Dan meets with Campus Pride, Shane tells his organization that they will be suspending any further protests against Chick-fil-A in light of this new understanding.

Later, toward the end of the year, Shane gets a message from Dan inviting him to be his personal guest at the Chick-fil-A Bowl on New Year's Eve.

It's game day. Two new friends with two different perspectives attend the event together. The game ends. The crowd parts. Two friends hug good-bye.

It's a new year.

Shane wrote an article in the *Huffington Post* in 2013 about the unlikely friendship that emerged between him and Dan. Throughout their conversations, they gained insight into each other's lives, values, and humanity. They found common ground: the importance of family. They bonded as friends with different lives, different values, and different beliefs, but with the same desire to see past the differences and into the person, the perspective, the heart.

Because there will always be differences of opinion in our world, progress doesn't have to mean persuasion. Progress can be as simple as caring enough to listen for understanding first before expecting to be understood. It can be as easy as a smile and a willingness to make new friends.

What matters about authentic leadership isn't the profit our businesses reap as a result, but the genuine connections and mutual acceptance of differences that can arise from renewed transparency.

What matters is the respect we have for others.

Perspectives
Value Reflection

Do you have friends or family whose political, religious, and/or lifestyle views are contrary to yours?

Do you at least understand why they believe they are right?

Do you respect them any less than you respect friends or family who share similar political, religious, or lifestyle views?

Do you ever feel threatened by opposing viewpoints? If so, why?

When was the last time you sincerely asked someone why they think the way they do? Did you argue with them? Did you learn something new?

Integrity

I look for three things in people. The first is personal integrity, the second is intelligence, and the third is a high energy level. But, if you don't have the first, the other two will kill you.

-Warren Buffett, CEO, Berkshire Hathaway

Chapter Seven

Agreements

*Determine that a thing can and shall be done, and then
we shall find the way.*

- Abraham Lincoln

Franchising is a model that is unique in the business world. It presents its own challenges and blessings compared to other business models. Arguably, the greatest blessing of franchising is the franchisees, and our franchisees are no exception.

Every year, The Dwyer Group holds an annual Reunion, a convention for our franchisees of all of our brands to unite with us under the same roof. Reunion is a chance for The Dwyer Group to show appreciation to our franchisees in person, something we take to heart. With more than sixteen hundred franchisees and growing, organizing an event for even a percentage of them can be a challenge in itself.

Although we didn't have as many franchisees back then as we do today, the 2004 Reunion was no exception.

A Dinner for Top Guns

Debbie reviews the itinerary once more. *Top Gun Dinner.* The event she and several others scheduled for the "Top Gun" franchisees—the top-performing franchisees of the year—is bound to be a hit. The outdoor Texas-themed dinner they've spent several months planning for includes games, dance lessons, a mechanical bull, armadillo races, bingo, and a wide variety of food. For the past several weeks, all of the Top Gun franchisees have been hearing the exciting details of the games, food, and events planned just for them.

She looks outside. The dark gray clouds seem to grow thicker by the second, eclipsing the sun. The weather forecasts are non-committal, unsure of the fate to come.

Debbie and several others who planned the dinner get into her Ford Excursion to drive toward the Rio Cibolo Ranch, in San Antonio, to prepare for the arrival of the franchisees. Before they even get to the ranch, the rains become a torrential downpour. Cars on the side of the road are stuck in floods up to the windows.

She steers cautiously through the entrance of the ranch. The winds are yanking leaves off the trees and the water slowly rises above the grass. As they drive past the flooded outdoor dance floor they realize it's time for plan B.

Except there is no plan B.

"Guys, we've got to find a way to give these franchisees a party tonight. We can't let them down," Debbie tells the group.

An associate in the backseat says, "But won't the franchisees understand if we postpone the event a day? I mean, all they have to do is look outside."

Debbie shakes her head. "No, you don't understand. Do you know how hard they've worked all year serving their customers? This one event is a way for us to serve them in return. It doesn't matter whether or not the franchisees would understand if we postponed the event; we told them we would give them dinner and a good time, so we're going to give it to them. Okay?"

"You're right," the associate says. "We need to make this dinner happen." Everyone else agrees.

Debbie turns the car around and pulls out her cell phone. She calls each of the bus drivers. "The ranch is flooded," she tells them. "Turn around and take the franchisees back to the hotel."

When they get back, she calls a local restaurant, Steers & Beers. The phone rings. A man answers. "Hello, my name is Debbie. We had an event planned at Rio Cibolo Ranch but it's flooded. Would you be able to serve 250 people chicken and steak within the next hour?"

"Uhh, I'll have to check on it. Can I call you right back?"

Debbie looks at her watch repeatedly, the second hand moving slower than ever. *Two hundred and fifty people are waiting for a dinner we promised them. We just can't let them down.*

The phone rings. *Please say yes, please say yes.* "Hello?"

"Hi, Debbie. We can have the food prepared, but there's just one problem."

"What is it?"

"We don't have enough servers."

She sighs in relief. This is the least of her worries at this point. "That's not a problem at all. We will help out! See you in an hour."

She rounds up executives, department and company heads, vice presidents, and assistants as well as a few willing franchisees. They all work together to serve drinks and food and to help clean tables. The owner of the restaurant set up karaoke for the franchisees.

After dinner is nearly finished, the owner informs Debbie that they don't have enough desserts. She rushes back to the hotel, goes to each of the restaurants, and arranges to have all of their desserts delivered to the franchisees.

It's two a.m. and several franchisees are still enjoying themselves. Most have already left, having thanked and congratulated the team for pulling off a hit. Debbie pays the owner handsomely and tips the restaurant staff for their hard work. She tells everyone it's time to leave. Although everyone is exhausted, they worked hard to make this night a success.

Debbie smiles. *It's just another great year at Reunion.*

Five Star Values

In 2015, we acquired a new franchise called Five Star Painting. We chose to purchase the franchise for many reasons, including their franchisees' values. These values have attracted values-driven franchisees, like Scott. Before we acquired the franchise, he told us about a customer situation that had happened where he allowed his personal values to decide the outcome:

We recently had a customer situation that was a little unique. The customer is an elderly woman who called us to get an estimate for a project. Once she felt comfortable enough with me and the estimate, I asked her where she lives so that we could come to her house and give her a final quote. She was hesitant to tell us but finally gave us her address.

When we arrived at her lakefront home, she told us about several fixes her husband had done around their house to save on cost. She shared with us that he had died two years ago. I realized why she had so much trepidation with telling us where she lived and why she needed to feel comfortable with us coming to her home. She lives alone and she has to trust that the contractors she hires are honest and will do the right thing.

The customer ended up hiring us for her paint and wood repair project. But as the work progressed, our team noticed a lot more wood rot that was not detected, nor could be detected, from the initial estimate. The estimate we had given her was around $10,000. Now, the wood rot would add an additional $4,000 to her bill. I called her to explain her situation, detailing all of the pieces that need to be replaced as well as the high cost of her siding. She agreed to the new charges and completed the project with good reviews.

However, toward the end of the project she wanted us to paint over her rotted deck railing. Several years ago, her husband had removed one of the railings on the bottom deck and moved it to the top deck. At this point, the bottom deck didn't have a railing at all. The railing was for an upper and lower deck around 200-feet long and 30-feet off the ground. It was unsafe and the additional charge to repair and paint over it would have been very high. Although our painter is skilled in deck railing repair we declined the additional work because we felt it was best to have a licensed general contractor manage this portion of her project. I explained the situation to her and referred her to a contractor we trust.

Our painter is a skilled tradesman and the customer would have paid us, but in the end we just did not feel comfortable that we were trained enough to meet all of the city codes that would need to be followed. We felt it was more important to enter into agreements that we can fully implement and warranty.

The Cost of Breaking Promises

Companies play a significant role in the lives of people today. Good employers understand the level of responsibility they have to their employees in this regard. So it should come as no surprise that studies have shown that when employers break promises to employees, it has a significant impact on the organization and the employees. Negative effects include:

- Decreased job satisfaction

- Decreased organizational commitment

- Decreased work performance

- Increased employee burnout

- Increased employee turnover

- Increased deviant behavior

Even the perception of promises broken by employers is enough to increase the likelihood of these effects among employees.

Although it is important to make only promises one is willing, able, and intends to keep, people are by no means perfect, and not every circumstance can be foreseen. So what happens when we know we can't live up to a promise or agreement we made?

Agreements
Value Reflection

How often do you promise to do something?

What percentage of the time would you say that you make good on your promises?

When was the last time someone promised you something and then broke or dismissed the promise? How did it make you feel?

When was the last time you were skeptical about a promise someone made and then he or she followed through? How did it make you feel?

Chapter Eight

Communication

We promise according to our hopes and perform according to our fears.

—François de La Rochefoucauld, French author, 1613-1680

Smartphones. Tablets. Computers. We are more connected than ever. And yet, we've lost the human connection. By the time you read this, people are likely already using wearable devices such as optical head-mounted displays (like Google Glass) and smartwatches (like Apple Watch). In ten years, these new technologies will be obsolete, replaced with newer, more inventive and integrative ones. As a society, we have chosen to become "faster" and "smarter." But in reality, all we've done is become more automated, with information more accessible than ever.

What has this done to our culture? Our lives? Our values? For many of us, it's hard to imagine how we used to live without a phone at our fingertips, or the world's knowledge available from our computers. Even harder is to imagine a life without phones or computers or data backup at all. We have taken for granted the fact that before all of these technologies, we had to research to find information, and truly connect with others in person. Even pre-Internet, we had to read books to find out what we wanted to know and we had to make plans in person or over the house phone or pay phone. When making agreements with people—like when and where to meet someone, or setting a deadline—we had to verbalize those agreements in person or leave a note. If we couldn't keep our agreement due to changing circumstances, we had to verbalize those changes in person or in writing.

How Technology Changes Values

It's important to stress the differences between societal values Pre- and Post-Internet. Let's consider a scenario. Pre-Internet, if we failed to verbalize changing circumstances that altered an original agreement with someone in person and in time, we were (hopefully) forgiven. However, if we consistently and regularly failed to verbalize changing circumstances in person and in time, we were understandably perceived as untrustworthy. Again we come to trustworthiness—*trust*. Not only is trust the foundation of strong values, but it is also the basis of any strong relationship and of meaningful communication. Post-Internet, we are on the cusp of taking this for granted.

How Technology Changes Relationships

In today's workforce, the impact of technology is most noticeable. At work, we use words less to form connections and more to transmit thoughts and ideas. Our business partners, managers, coworkers, vendors, clients and customers—how much do we know them? Care about them? Trust them? Do we share similar values with them?

Are these people we interact with, or are they names in an inbox?

It seems that we don't have time for the things that used to be necessary to make businesses run. We don't have time to walk across the office to schedule a meeting with someone. We don't have time to finish one project on time, because we're already on to the next. The world is moving at breakneck speed and we're struggling so hard to keep up, we almost don't even notice it anymore. Did we invent technology to help us keep up, or did the technology we invented give us the capability to move faster than we can handle?

Does it matter?

How We've Become

We use e-mails and text messages in place of phone calls and face-to-face conversations. We use digital calendars to remind us of appointments, meetings, deadlines. We use smartphones and social media to remember people's names, phone numbers, e-mail addresses, and even faces.

Because of the combination of instant communication and less in-person interaction, we can ask for more from more people but not know their workloads because we never see them *at* work. As a result, we have more meetings, more deadlines, more to-dos than ever before in human history, and we do all of this with the power of artificially lit screens. We are less in touch with each other and we live more often inside our heads. This was exhibited as early as 1998 in a study of the workplace in which employees who attend meetings on a regular basis admitted to:

- Daydreaming (91 percent)

- Missing meetings (96 percent)

- Missing parts of meetings (95 percent)

But the most startling finding in this study was that 73 percent admitted to bringing other work with them to a meeting.

Where Do We Go from Here?

Communication is a major problem in most businesses today. We're sharing information faster than we can process it. We're moving faster than we can talk. Although many people pride themselves on their "multitasking abilities," humans are not natural multitaskers.

We use communication channels to share more of our thoughts and ideas than ever. And yet, we've lost the human aspect of communication. Technology is not going away anytime soon. Although it has enhanced so much of our lives (when was the last time you used a paper map on a road trip?), it has also presented us with a new set of challenges and changes. We must learn how to adapt technology to our values, not adapt our values to technology.

At The Dwyer Group, one value in our Code of Values is that we *communicate any potentially broken agreements at the first appropriate opportunity to all parties concerned.* This reminds us that we should be proactive in communicating with stakeholders when plans or promises change. This can be difficult in a fast-paced work environment, but it is important; it ensures that each of us has the information we need to keep up with the pace of the company and the world.

But there is a deeper, core value that lies beneath this one. It's not just about "keeping tabs"; rather, it's about earning and keeping trust in a world that is trust starved. After all, if we can't earn and keep trust in today's society and workforce, then how can we expect the person on the other side of that backlit, digital screen to do the same? And would values still matter?

Communication
Value Reflection

Has anyone ever stared at their phone, tablet, or computer while you were trying to talk to them? Were they actively listening? How did it make you feel? How often do you do this to other people?

The next time you eat at a restaurant, count the number of people *not dining alone* who are looking at their smartphones or tablets. Are you surprised by this number? Share your findings with someone.

As you reflect on these things, do you think technology makes us more productive or more busy? Does technology help us with or distract us from letting someone know that we will be late to a meeting or late turning in a project?

Chapter Nine

System Correction

Think not those faithful who praise all thy words and actions, but those who kindly reprove thy faults.

- Socrates

People are lined up in rows between metal dividers, awaiting their turn. Some are talking at a rapid pace with friends and family. Others are silent, absentmindedly chewing their nails and bouncing a leg. Echoes of distant screams flood the tunnel in front of them. The ground tremors and rattles forcefully, like thunder beneath their feet. The screaming happens again, but louder. Closer. Then it stops. A *whoosh* comes from the left side of the tunnel and the people know their turn is almost here.

The gates swing open like cattle pens.

People file into the roller coaster cars. In 52 years, Rosy has never been one to shy away from adventure. Anticipation builds. This is a good day to have fun with her family. The ride safety operators walk up and down the sides of the cars, lowering the restraint bars into a locked position above the riders' thighs. Rosy is seated by herself. She feels unsure of how well the restraint is locked. Just to make sure, she catches the attention of a young attendant and expresses her concern that she's not properly restrained. He reassures her, "As long as you heard it click, you're fine."

The ride attendant announces the beginning of the ride over a microphone. The track hisses and the cars move forward. Rosy's daughter and son-in-law are in the seats in front of her. Her son is in another car she cannot see. The chains *click-click-click* beneath them as they are towed up the steep incline. This ride stakes claim to being the world's steepest roller coaster track with a 95-degree record-breaking bank after a fourteen-story ascent.

As they reach the top of the 150-foot hill, the ride creeps slowly for a moment just before falling forward. Gravity yanks them down the slope at freefall. The riders float upward in their seats, held back from oblivion only by their restraints.

Gleeful screams.

Within seconds, they are at the bottom. Lungs, limbs, stomachs drop, avalanching downward at the bottom of the hill from the sudden shift in direction. Rosy hears a loud *pop* as her restraint loosens. Over the hill, at the next steep drop off, she yells. She is flying upwards, away from the car, the track. Away from safety.

Panicked screams.

When the ride is over, Rosy's family runs off the ride. "She fell," the son shouts. "She fell!" Quickly down the stairs. Hurry. Screaming, "Mom! Mom!" Her son climbs the fence and falls over. He rights himself and sprints somewhere, anywhere. "Mom!" Frantic. Adrenaline. Park security runs like a mob toward him. "My mom! She fell! We need to go get her!"

Terrified screams.

Unforeseen

Rosy died on impact from the fall on July 19, 2013 at Six Flags Over Texas in Arlington, Texas. Freak accidents such as this are horrific and devastating to the lives and businesses that surround them. In some cases, they are preventable--especially if you respond appropriately and quickly to the tragedy--but they are almost always unforeseen and unintended.

Most businesses do not risk facing such catastrophic mistakes or broken systems. In all businesses, however, the importance of response time and how the response is handled are virtually the same. The key is to use mistakes or other issues as opportunities for improvement. To do this, you have to look at the system and identify the cause, and then correct the system after thinking through all of the potential solutions.

Six Flags responded immediately to the incident and to Rosy's tragic death in a written statement:

> *We are deeply saddened to share that earlier this evening an adult woman died in the park while on the Texas Giant. Park medical staff and local paramedics responded immediately. Since the safety of our guests and employees is our number one priority, the ride has been closed pending further investigation. Our thoughts and prayers are with the family and friends during this difficult time.*

Later, the spokeswoman for Six Flags, Shannon Parker, said in a written statement, "We are working closely with authorities to determine the cause of the accident." And, indeed, in the months that followed, the company put their promises into action. After extensive investigations and testing (both internal and external), Six Flags Over Texas was cleared by the Texas Department of Insurance to reopen the ride without further safety concerns.

Take it to Heart

Sometimes the best way to prevent mistakes is to proactively find areas that need improvement. At The Dwyer Group we are in the business of franchising and great systems are one of the main ingredients for the success of any franchise business (or any business, for that matter). But no system is perfect. That's why every year The Dwyer Group sends out a survey to franchisees asking them several questions regarding their overall satisfaction. In the 90's, however, we would survey franchisees over the phone because most of them did not have e-mail yet. Employees throughout the company would be assigned a group of franchisees to call and ask them some questions about their experiences with our company. A franchisee I spoke to, who has been with one of our companies for a long time, gave me some very honest feedback. She did so knowing that we would take it to heart and take the necessary steps to improve our systems.

She informed me that she was not satisfied with the response time from her franchise coach. Her former franchise coach always responded to her questions or concerns in a timely fashion. She did say, however, that when her new franchise coach did reply, he did an excellent job of answering her questions thoroughly and was obviously knowledgeable and experienced. But often it took her days to get answers when sometimes it was important to get a swift response.

She also told me that she was a little reluctant to share this frustration because she did not want to get this person in trouble. She reiterated that he really was good at his job, but just needed to significantly improve his timeliness. After she told me all of this, I thanked her and told her not to worry about him getting in trouble. I wanted her to know that it was because of her feedback that I was able to look to the system for correction and that we would do so immediately.

I happened to know this particular franchise coach and he was new to the team. I knew that we had hired him because of his strong technical background and that we had loaded him up with many projects because of his expertise. I scheduled some time to speak with him about his situation. We discussed his challenge of responding in a timely fashion. He acknowledged that we had put higher priority on his projects due to some tight deadlines. This in turn prevented him from responding in a timely fashion to some franchisees. In looking at the big picture, we made the decision to clarify that responding to the franchisees' needs should always take priority over projects. To take the pressure off of this coach we moved back the deadlines for his assignments. This allowed him to deliver on the promise of our priority to respond to our franchisees as quickly as possible.

One of the things I've learned as a leader at The Dwyer Group is that when something is not going right in our business we need to look at ourselves first, as leaders, before we point the finger at anyone else. In this case, The Dwyer Group needed to look at its system to identify areas that needed to be improved. Learning opportunities like this have been the motivation we needed to put a better self-improvement system in place. That's why one of the habits we've created is to ask these questions:

1. Do we have a system in place to prevent this challenge from happening again?

2. If we do, then let's do a better job of training to the system.

3. If we don't, then let's create an efficient system and train accordingly.

Corrective Measures

When we make a mistake, we have to do more than just acknowledge it. In the case of Six Flags, there were several steps to making the corrections necessary to get to the point where the ride was safe enough to reopen. The president of Six Flags Over Texas, Steve Martindale, released a statement on the date of the reopening:

> We added incremental and overlapping safety measures to the ride including re-designed lap-bar restraint pads and seat belts. We also added a test seat at the ride-line entrance so guests can determine if they properly fit in the restraint system … We continue to extend our deepest condolences to [Rosy's]

family … This was a tragic accident that deeply affected our employees, especially since safety is our highest priority and at the heart of everything we do.

Although this tragedy could not be predicted, Six Flags did not waste any time realizing that there was a process they needed to fix in order to prevent such incidents in the future. At no point did Six Flags blame the rider. They knew that the responsibility to ensure the safety of their guests is, at the end of the day, their number one priority.

In any business, there is ample opportunity to deny responsibility for mistakes or to simply ignore them. If Six Flags had denied any responsibility for the accident, or had not given it the serious attention it deserved, would they have been able to maintain the trust of their customers?

System Correction
Value Reflection

Have you ever been a part of, or affected by, what you considered to be a broken system? Did you speak up about it? If not, why?

Have you ever proposed an alternate solution to a problem or a broken process? Was your proposal implemented? If so, how did it turn out? If not, how did that make you feel?

What workplace, school, church, or governmental systems do you think are broken or ineffective? Why? Do you have a solution? Have you told anyone?

What is one system you're passionate about fixing? What can you do this week to work toward a solution?

Chapter Ten

Accountability

The individual is not accountable to society for his actions insofar as these actions concern the interests of no person but himself.

- John Stuart Mill, British philosopher and economist, 1806-1873

Twelve-year-old Mary Kellerman shuffles into her parents' bedroom in her pajamas. The soft glow of dawn diffusing through the window glides along her face as she walks up to their bed. It's six thirty in the morning on a school day, and she tells her parents she doesn't feel well. Her throat hurts and she sniffles, fighting a runny nose. Her parents open a new bottle of extra-strength Tylenol and give her one. Several minutes pass. Young Mary walks into the bathroom. She shuts the door. Her father hears the sound of something heavy dropping to the floor.

"Mary, are you okay?" he asks loudly. No response. This time more loudly: "Mary? Are you okay?"

Silence. He walks to the bathroom door and opens it. Little Mary is in a heap on the floor. She is still, quiet, unconscious.

Hers is just the first of several similar tragic events to come that day.

September 29, 1982 - 12:00 P.M.

Adam's young children just finished the lunch he made them. He's taking a sick day from his job at the post office. "I'm going to take two Tylenol and lie down," he tells his family. He disappears into the back of the house.

Minutes pass. His wife is cleaning the kitchen. She turns around. Adam has returned, his eyes wide, panting and struggling to get a full breath. He begins shaking. He sways as he takes a few steps. He wilts and falls forward.

3:45 P.M.

Mary Reiner just had her fourth child a week ago. The exhaustion of caring for an infant seems to get harder with each child, especially when she's responsible for all four while her husband is finishing up a day at work to make ends meet. Mary's exhaustion overtakes her. She gets up to take some Tylenol.

Eight year-old Michelle hears her mother's strenuous breathing from the other room. She walks toward the room where Mary is, the panting growing louder with each step. She turns a corner and sees her mother trembling before falling to the floor.

Johnson & Johnson

A group of employees are huddled over a speakerphone. Minutes before, the reporter on the other end of the line asked for the company's comment on the sudden deaths of several people in Chicago, all connected to the use of extra-strength Tylenol. One of the men has his hand over his mouth, unaware of his pose, his eyebrows arched and his stare distant. The other men's faces wear a similar pained expression.

"As we said, sir, this is the first we are hearing of this," one of the men tells the reporter. Another man leans to the person beside him and whispers, "We've got to tell James." The man beside him turns and leaves.

James Burke, CEO

"We've got to recall it." James's voice is resolute and his thoughts troubled by the suddenness of the situation: innocent lives stolen by the very product he's spent years marketing. The company's legal counsel sits across from him, flustered by dismissed advice.

"Listen, James," one of them says, "the police think a madman has been lacing our pills with cyanide. With all due respect, if we recall Tylenol now, the public will get the perception that one crazy person can bring a major corporation to its knees."

James places his knuckles on the desk and leans forward. "No, *you* listen. We don't know how widespread the contaminated Tylenol is or isn't. Saving the product is important, but what's far more important is protecting the people. Am I clear?" His gaze is locked on the lawyers. They dare not retort. "Good. Now, I want you to set up toll-free customer support hotlines and get as many employees as possible to man the lines. I also need you to assemble a seven-person team to help me decide on the best strategy to fix this problem quickly."

The Seven

It's only coincidence that seven people were assembled at Johnson & Johnson to investigate the most ethical response to what ended up being seven total deaths from premeditated cyanide poisoning. With James leading the group, the company's first response was an extensive nationwide media platform to alert consumers to immediately stop using Tylenol. They also announced that the company had stopped the production and advertising of all Tylenol products and was in the process of removing all bottles from stores in Chicago and the surrounding areas. Simultaneously, they sent the same message to more than 450,000 doctors' offices and hospitals.

Not long after the media campaign, James and his team collaborated with the FDA and FBI and told the government representatives that they strongly recommended the removal and destruction of all thirty-two million bottles of Tylenol across the country.

"How much is this going to cost the company?" executives asked him.

"I don't know," he said, "and it doesn't matter. Doing the right thing is the only thing that matters."

James would later find out that doing the right thing—the ethical thing—would cost the company $100 million. It's a bitter pill for any company to swallow, but, as James would agree, there is no price tag on human lives.

Tamper Resistant

In the wake of the murders and the nationwide recall, Johnson & Johnson immediately headed back to the drawing board to develop the world's first tamper-resistant bottle. Press releases and media appearances revealed to the nation the glued box, the plastic cover around the lid, and the foil seal. Coupons also ran in newspapers across the country for $2.50 off the new triple-sealed bottles of Tylenol.

Over the following weeks, representatives gave more than 2,250 presentations across the medical industry to reassure medical professionals that Tylenol is a safe product. The company worked hard toward recovering Johnson & Johnson's market value drop of more than $1 billion.

And all these steps ultimately worked. Customers were comforted by the company's humane and sympathetic response. Five months later, the company had regained 70 percent of its market share. Today, tamper-resistant bottles are used by manufacturers of over-the-counter medicine; Johnson & Johnson changed the industry for the better because they refused to give up on what mattered most: people *first*.

"It's our responsibility to . . ."

James Burke always took the company's code of ethics very seriously. Its message of corporate responsibility never left his mind as he led the government toward public safety and Johnson & Johnson toward recovery and growth. A part of the company's code of ethics reads:

It's our responsibility to ensure all company-based, medically relevant product information is fair and balanced, accurate and comprehensive, to enable well-informed risk-benefit assessments about our products.

It's our responsibility to understand differences in values across cultures and to adapt our behaviors in keeping with our ethical principles.

It's our responsibility to challenge each other regarding medical and ethical concerns.

James Burke's ethical, values-driven leadership is still being written about in today's business textbooks. His leadership earned him the distinction of being one of "History's 10 Greatest CEOs" in *Fortune* magazine in 2003. In 2000, it also earned him the honor of receiving the Presidential Medal of Freedom. Although James died in 2012, he has left a legacy of virtuosity in business that still resonates today. He died on September 28, the day before the thirtieth anniversary of the "Tylenol Murders." Murders by a killer who is still unknown and uncaught.

How to Apologize

Values-driven leaders and organizations are never afraid to apologize and don't see remorse as a sign of weakness. Leaders with the outmoded perception that authority and power are the foundation of leadership are more likely to forget what truly matters. They've forgotten that humility and hubris are endpoints on a spectrum of ego. In fact, in his book *Good to Great*, Jim Collins shows that consistently high-performing companies tend to be led by "Level 5" leadership. These are leaders who exhibit humility, fairness, and utilitarian qualities. In other words, they set their focus more on the mission and the well-being and perspectives of other people than on themselves and the bottom line. They also are quick to think about the potential long-term consequences or benefits of their decisions. Because of these things, they lead their companies toward superior financial performance as a result of their values-driven leadership and earn their followers' trust and respect.

So how should leaders and organizations hold themselves accountable for their mistakes? The way anyone should: Immediately own the mistakes, apologize, and find the best way to make amends. Hershey H. Friedman is a researcher who has done a thorough audit of studies in apologizing. He found that good apologies have four key elements:

1. Acknowledging the mistake or offense.

2. Communicating remorse for the mistake or offense and exhibiting behaviors that show signs of regret or shame, humility, and sincerity.

3. Explaining why the mistake or offense happened.

4. Offering reparations/restitution.

Accountability and apologies lead to trust. However, despite the positive results of trust, research shows that trust in management within companies is low and continues to decline.

Leaders Are Carved Out

Leaders with high visibility within an organization or community are beset by higher expectations from followers than those of lower-visibility leaders. Joanne Ciulla, a researcher on the subject of imperfect leaders, reminds us that leaders are "carved out of the warped wood of humanity." Remembering this is the first step toward admitting our faults. It's also the first step to accepting the apologies of others.

So why is it so hard for us to remember our imperfections? For the scientific answer, we turn to research in the field of social psychology. The findings of multiple studies have revealed:

- We work hard to keep up a positive self-concept in our private and public worlds.

- People want to perceive themselves as moral, deserving, and honest.

- Eighty-four percent of people report that they are moral people and that their morality is exhibited in their private and public lives.

- People tend to recall their good behavior more easily and tend to forget their unethical behavior.

- Sometimes people justify their actions to lessen the severity of their unethical behavior. Such justifications include things like blaming external pressures, claiming the behavior is for the greater good, or referring to the fact that other people are "doing it too."

- People adjust the definition or interpretation of their own values in order to justify their behavior.

Another area that has a wealth of research is moral hypocrisy. This is the tendency of people to judge themselves leniently and others more severely. Sometimes, the selfish outlook on success can lead to moral hypocrisy. Rationalization of unethical behavior and a sense of entitlement can get the better of successful and otherwise good people. Take President Nixon and the Watergate scandal, for instance. During his news conference, Nixon insisted, "People have got to know whether or not their president is a crook. Well, I'm not a crook. I've earned everything I've got."

The rationalizations and moral hypocrisy of company leadership and their unwillingness to admit their mistakes have a far more negative impact than admitting and apologizing. In fact, such hypocrisy causes disenchantment throughout the company, poor decision making, low learning in employees, and poor company performance. But when leaders are accountable for their actions, they think of others more and will place the interest and well-being of others above their own.

Some of the world's greatest leaders in the past century, such as Nelson Mandela, Martin Luther King Jr., Mother Teresa, and Mahatma Gandhi, are human like the rest of us. Each of them is carved from the same "warped wood" as we are. Undoubtedly their high visibility helped to keep them accountable, but if they made a mistake, they would apologize. Even if they weren't as widely known, they would do the right thing anyway. Aren't they some of the greatest role models for the values of love, kindness, and honesty?

Accountability
Value Reflection

When was the last time you made a major
mistake? Did you accept responsibility?
Did you apologize?

When was the last time someone made a major
mistake that had a significant impact on you? Do
you know who did it? Did he or she apologize, or
not? How did that make you feel?

Have you ever made a mistake that you've never
admitted to? What was it? Why didn't you admit
to it? Whom did it affect?

What is one negative behavior that you know you
need to improve? Whom does that behavior hurt?
Today, apologize to that person and ask him or
her how you can work to fix the behavior.

Chapter Eleven

Honesty

I hope I shall possess firmness and virtue enough to maintain what I consider the most enviable of all titles, the character of an honest man.

- George Washington

The heat and humidity of midsummer in Western India make the journey of several miles last an eternity. But for a young mother desperate to help her son, even an eternity in summer can't outlast her love.

"Mummy, why do we have to walk so far?"

"Because, my son, no matter how many times I or the doctors tell you to stop eating sweets, you won't listen."

The young boy looks up at his mother, his eyebrows drawn together in confusion. "But, Mummy, I like sweets."

"Yes, child," she sighs. "I know you do. But you are diabetic and the sweets make you sick." She stops and kneels in front of her son. Her hands cup his face; her thumbs stroke his small cheeks. Tears well up as she stares at him.

"What's wrong, Mummy?"

The mother chuckles in awe at the kindheartedness of her child. She wraps her arms around him and pulls him close. His little hands pat her shoulders.

They continue their journey in silence. When they arrive at the edge of the city, they hear a crowd cheering in the near distance. As the mother and her child round the corner of a building, they see hundreds of men, women, and children flocking around a small man. The young mother smiles—they have arrived just in time.

"Come, child, we must hurry!" She clutches the boy's hand and they run toward the crowd. She leads the boy through the back of the crowd, sidestepping and weaving through a forest of healthy and oblivious people.

The boy falls and their hands separate. "Mummy!"

The mother turns around and sees her son in flashes through the movement of the crowd. She runs to him and reaches out. "Grab my hand, child!" He cleaves to her hand. She says to him, "Now, quick! He will be leaving soon!"

As she gets closer to the edge of the crowd she begins to catch glimpses of the man. Her heart surges. "Mahatma ji!" she cries. He cannot hear her. She shouts even louder, "Mahatma ji!" He turns his head. She breaks through the crowd and steps forward. Gandhi approaches with the aid of his walking stick, peers through his round wire glasses, and smiles wide when he sees the young mother and her son.

Breathless from running through the crowd, she pants as she begins to speak. "Mahatma ji, I have come to you with a matter of serious concern to me. My son is diabetic and he eats too many sweets." Gandhi looks at the boy with a smile, his own front teeth missing. "He won't stop," she continues, "no matter how much the doctors or I ask him to stop. It is making him very sick and I am worried for his health. My son respects you greatly and if you tell him to stop, he will listen."

"I see," Gandhi says, his voice soft and gentle. His mind is lost in concentration as he looks at the child, leaning on the walking stick with both hands. Then, he looks at the young mother and says, "You are a good mother and your boy is very precious. Please come back to me in a week and I will speak to him." He smiles genially and, hands together, bows to her. She bows back but cannot hide her confused and disappointed expression.

A week later, the mother and her son arrive early to see Mahatma Gandhi. When he arrives, she rushes toward him amid the throng, carrying her son in her arms. "Mahatma ji!" she shouts, "It is I, the mother of the diabetic child!" Gandhi turns around and smiles.

"Your son and I must have a little talk," he says. He holds out his hand and says to the boy, "Come, child." They walk several feet away. Gandhi places his hand on the boy's face as he speaks quietly to him. The young mother cannot make out what Gandhi is saying to the boy, but she sees her son nodding. Gandhi brings the talk to a close by patting the boy's cheek gently and chuckling.

The boy runs back to her and clutches her sari. He says to her, "Mummy, Gandhi spoke to me and I promised that I would stop eating sweets." She is overjoyed and cannot hold back the tears. She gets on her knees to hug him tightly.

She stands again and says to Gandhi, "Thank you, Mahatma ji! Thank you!" But the memory of last week returns to her. "Forgive me, Mahatma ji, but why did you ask us to wait a whole week? Why did you not speak to my son then?"

Gandhi chuckles and says, "I myself have always loved sweets and have always eaten more than I should. I asked you to return to me in a week because I could not tell your son to do something that I was not willing to give up until that moment. Therefore, I had to commit to stop eating sugar before I could ask your son to do the same."

They share a moment of understanding and joyful silence. Gandhi puts his hands together and bows before walking off into the noisy crowd.

This retelling of a touching story about Gandhi's willingness to change himself before he could ask others to change is a powerful testament to his profound honesty. Not only was Gandhi a political and civil rights leader for the people of India, but he has been an inspiration for people around the world. His call for nonviolence both in everyday life and in revolutions has inspired such people as Martin Luther King Jr. and Nelson Mandela.

But to many, Gandhi was more than just a civil rights leader; he was a spiritual leader as well. I believe this is because of his willingness to lead by example and to never allow himself to contradict his values, even in the face of violence or death. He is an example of the ultimate values-driven leader.

Values-Driven Leaders

As we've already established, everyone is a leader—it's *what kind* of leader that is called into question. This book is written to inspire as many people as possible to be values-driven leaders. People trust values-driven leaders. Why? Because the core of being a values-driven leader, whether at work or at home or elsewhere, is not only the demonstration of love for people, but honesty as well. (I speak of honesty in the sense of being truthful and true to oneself and one's values.) Few people are willing to follow the example of someone who won't speak out against actions that oppose the values they stand for.

Two researchers, Jim Kouzes and Barry Posner, found in their studies that "followers follow character and character begins with honesty and integrity." They also found that of all the characteristic qualities of great leaders, followers admire and value honesty the most. Their studies have carried them around the world to research many different cultures and people. They discovered that honesty (rated as integrity and trustworthiness in their studies) was the number one quality of a leader that is most likely to inspire followers to follow willingly, with the least amount of apprehension. Followers pay attention to the consistency of a leader's behavior to help measure the honesty of that leader. Kouzes and Posner's findings are true whether the leader in question is at a company, at home, at school or church, or a leader in the public domain.

Leaders who do speak up for the values they believe in are likely to find far more people to re-sound their beliefs. Take Gandhi and Martin Luther King Jr. as examples—both men spoke up against great injustices, both led millions to stand up for their basic rights in the face of tyranny, and both spoke often about the virtue of nonviolent dissent. Then and now they were hailed as brave leaders and exemplary measures of how to live one's life, because they stood up even when it was unpopular. Their values resonated with many and stood in opposition to the values of many others. This is the mark of a great leader, one with staying power—a values-driven leader.

Speak Up, Even When It Is Difficult

Like most people in America, I have been a passive participant in a game of football during many Super Bowls. For many, football is an all-American pastime, and we sit in front of the TV for almost four hours, unwilling to miss a moment of the game. Because of this, Super Bowl commercials are some of the most expensive and lucrative forms of advertising. The NFL also holds a halftime show designed to hold your attention while the teams break in the middle of the game. The halftime show has taken on a following in its own right.

In 2013, for example, Nielsen ratings reported that the halftime show was seen by 110.8 million viewers, which, at the time, made it the second-most watched halftime show in Super Bowl history. The performance had Twitter followers abuzz, generating

268,000 tweets *per minute*, making it the most tweeted event in history at the time.

Critics responded to this performance with great acclaim. Melinda Newman, of the entertainment news website HitFix, said, "In a Super Bowl half-time performance that was as frenetic as it was fierce, [she] delivered a sexy segment that was part [lingerie] fashion show, part tutorial on how to dazzle an audience." Rob Sheffield, of *Rolling Stone*, shared Melinda's perspective: "Now *that* was a halftime show, and *that* is a star. This woman single-handedly blew out the power in the Superdome. No special guests, no costume changes—just [her], her heels, her thighs, her leather-and-lace corset and a freewheeling romp through her songbook, ignoring most of her proven crowd-pleasers just because ... [she] can get away with doing whatever [she] feels like doing."

There's no question that these performances garner a lot of mostly positive attention, but there's also no question that they have a direct impact on the lives of hundreds of millions of viewers. The question is: What *kind* of impact?

I respect the artists and their talent during the Super Bowl halftime shows, but I have been deeply disappointed with some of the performances and with the NFL. The shows often further perpetuate the stereotypes that female artists must be scantily clad and overtly sexual in their performance to be taken seriously by an audience of primarily men. When I look at TV, movies, ads, magazines, and even lingerie catalogue covers, I can't help but ask, "Why are women still not taken seriously *as they are*?"

I also continue to be disappointed by the artists in the Super Bowl as leaders. Females of all ages, sizes, and cultures watch the kind of attention the artists receive. Whether it is intentional or not, men of all ages, sizes, and cultures are also fed yet another media display of fashion model bodies as an image for how women "should" look in order to be considered attractive. And as a leader of women (and men), shouldn't I stand up for the values I believe in? I decided to write a letter to the organizers of the halftime show to encourage them to have a more inspiring and patriotic show – a show that exemplifies the great values America was born with.

The memory of the Super Bowl halftime show and my response to it came back to the forefront of my mind as I received a catalogue in the mail from a popular lingerie company. Their products are of high quality, but as the years go by, the photos they've used seem to have become less about the products and more about the images of idealized and sexualized women. But I believe women are more than objects and more than their beauty! This time, I'd had enough. I called the company and explained my perspective. I also asked to be removed from the mailing list and the loyalty program. Although some people may not share my perspective on, or passion for, this topic, what matters is that people are all leaders, and leaders should speak up about their values and what matters to them.

A Personal Value: Empowering Women

People who saw my episode of *Undercover Boss* know that I believe in the strength and power of women. Without more female leaders, how will we combat the outdated stereotypes and image-obsessed culture? In the service industries that comprise The Dwyer Group brands, females are even more rare. That's why I was proud of Tanna, a front-line service professional of a Mr. Appliance franchise, when I met her on the show. She was smart and strong and worked hard to support her family. She also didn't have to alter her appearance to be taken seriously as a professional and an appliance repair technician. She was just Tanna: service professional, mother, and woman.

At the conclusion of that show, I invited Tanna to work with our corporate office to design a program to inspire more women to become professionals in the home service industry. The program is called Women in the Trades; The Dwyer Group offers scholarships to female applicants to trade schools in the home services industry. As the co-chair and former CEO of The Dwyer Group, I've worked hard to lead by example in order to inspire other women to become leaders in their lives and in their fields. Everyone is an example of their values to others; it's the quality of those values that determines the quality of leadership. The example you set for others is driven by the values behind the actions and decisions you make.

Executive Decisions

For many executives, it has taken years of power struggles and harsh decisions to get where they are. So it is no surprise that so many of them turn out to carry those behaviors with them into the executive suites and boardrooms. But such is not the case with Gerald McCaughey, the president and CEO of Canadian Imperial Bank of Commerce (CIBC).

In 2003, three executives of CIBC were involved with Enron in the manipulation of its financial statements. During the scandal that ensued, investors of CIBC won a settlement of $2.4 billion. At the time, Gerald was the new CEO of CIBC, and although he was not involved with the Enron scandal, he knew he had to earn the trust of the investors and the employees. As part of his transition, he decided to voluntarily accept a compensation package that would long delay any vesting of his stock in the company. He also included in the package the stipulation that his compensation would be rescinded retroactively if another scandal occurred at the bank during his term as CEO.

Integrity on the Green?

In 2002, Starwood Hotels did a study on executives who carry out business deals during a game of golf. What they found was in some respects humorous, but in most ways depressing:

- 59 percent of executives believe how a person plays golf is similar to how he or she conducts business

- 73 percent believe that how a person plays golf shows that person's "true" character

- 87 percent have played with someone who cheated

- 82 percent say they hate people who cheat when they play golf

- 82 percent of executives admit to cheating on the golf course

- 86 percent admit to cheating in business

In addition, 85 percent of these executives report feeling embarrassed by another person's bad behavior during a game. The worst behavior that they reported being witness to includes:

- vulgar and/or abusive language

- throwing or breaking clubs

- throwing clubs into a lake or pond

- excessive drinking

If we are all leaders who live our values by example, these executives' golf games are certainly revealing. It is clear what a person's character is when honesty is of no importance to him or her.

I can't imagine Gandhi doing these things during a game of golf, but if I imagine Gandhi being invited to play golf, I expect he would lean on his golf club with both hands and smile, saying something like, "I like this game—there's no tackling or blocking, only patience and persistence." In this way, doesn't values-driven change share the same characteristics as golf?

Honesty
Value Reflection

When was the last time you justified to yourself a lie that you told? Why did you justify it?

Have you ever known that someone was telling you a lie? Did you tell him or her you were aware that they were lying to you? If so, how did they respond? If not, why not?

Who is your greatest personal role model? How would it make you feel if he or she lied to you about something you felt was important?

When was the last time you were unfairly treated by someone who was being a hypocrite? Is there anything about yourself that you are also critical of in others? Be honest.

Chapter Twelve

Clarification

*The wise man doesn't give the right answers, he poses
the right questions.*

- *Claude Lévi-Strauss*

The number one cause of preventable tragic events in the medical industry—ahead of factors such as training, patient assessment, and competency—is communication. Or, rather, *mis*communication. Various forms of miscommunication in medicine lead to mistakes that could have been prevented with simple clarification. In fact, the issue of preventable medical errors is so particularly severe and tragic that it is the eighth leading cause of death in the U.S. The economic costs are also significant: In 2005, the cost of preventable mistakes in medicine was estimated to be between $17 billion and $29 billion per year.

Although the impact of miscommunication within the medical industry is arguably more severe than in most industries, are people who work in the medical field really more prone to mistakes than others? Are they simply careless?

Of course not. They are simply one of us: human. And humans have a propensity for miscommunication, it seems. History is rife with proof of wars and tragedies that have occurred due to a lack of understanding during communication. But most miscommunications, while frustrating or, at times, costly, fortunately do not have life-or-death outcomes.

People listen, on average, with only about 25 percent efficiency. Thoughts, ideas, and daydreams cloud our comprehension during communication. Even factors such as body language, tone of voice, our mood, our feelings about those we communicate with, and our worldview have an impact on the interpretation of messages we receive. It's not without irony, then, that a large study across several industries found that a majority of people believe themselves to be better communicators than their coworkers.

Other times, people come to an impasse during conversations when they simply disagree with each other. It's not a matter of misunderstanding in these cases, but rather the dichotomy of perspectives. It's in situations like this that communication is doubly important. As values-driven leaders, we must work to understand one another, and we can only get to such an understanding by talking *with*, and not *at*, each other. Even in disagreements in which frustrations have the potential to perpetuate a breakdown in communication, we are accountable for our reactions, so we must do all we can to listen before asking to be listened to.

The Red-Flag E-mail

During my first year as president and CEO of The Dwyer Group, in 1999, I made a personal goal to be accessible to employees, franchisees, and customers. Even in those days some people felt that CEOs were out of touch with reality (hence the success of Undercover Boss!), and I wanted to change that paradigm within our company. No one needs yes-men, and I'm no different. People hold CEOs accountable for the reality within their company. Sometimes that means the good things; other times it means the difficult things. An e-mail I got in my early months taught me this lesson.

Top Gun is a program that is very important to many of our franchisees. It is a target to strive for and a sense of recognition that they are following the system. It provides us an opportunity to reward them during our annual Reunion convention. But in the middle of the year, we had changed the revenue criteria to attain the Top Gun status. At the time, we didn't know it, but this change knocked one franchisee out of the running. And he made sure to clarify his perspective with us.

I had spent several days preparing for my first keynote address for Reunion, which would be held in Orlando, Florida, that year. I was nervous and excited at the same time. In the middle of preparations, I received Russ's e-mail.

The Dwyer Group had certain criteria for Top Gun, the e-mail began. *Well, right in the middle of the year, they said, "Okay, the criteria have changed. You now need X dollars or sales to make Top Gun."*

As I read his words, the room felt smaller, tighter. Doubt about my keynote presentation began whispering in my mind. But it was the truth of what he said that stood out: *Well, I just thought that was wrong. It's like a football game; you don't get halfway through the game and decide you're going to change the rules. Now, maybe next year they can change the criteria so that it's clearly spelled out and everyone knows up front. That would be okay. But not in the middle of the year.*

Russ was right, and I knew it. Even though I knew about the changes and had approved them, I simply hadn't thought about what it would be like for the franchisees in his situation. It was frustrating for Russ and other franchisees, as his closing statement made clear: *I will be in Orlando during Reunion, but I'll be in Disney World to visit the real Mickey Mouse.*

The e-mail was almost too painful to read.

Truth from the Field

I closed the e-mail, the words echoing in my mind. It wasn't long after that when Larry walked into my office holding a Code of Values card. Larry was from Mr. Rooter corporate and had been out in the field recently. He had visited Russ as the rule changes were taking place. Russ had clarifying questions for Larry, and Larry knew I would have clarifying questions too. He gave me a firsthand account of Russ's frustration and confusion.

"Russ felt that the new revenue levels clearly favor franchisees in bigger populations. He told me that he feels it's making it impossible for franchisees like him in smaller populations to make Top Gun. On top of that, changing the rules in the middle of the game was the last straw for him. And I completely understand his concerns, Dina." Larry pointed to the Code of Values. *We live our Code of Values by asking clarifying questions if we disagree or do not understand.* "It was because I understood his concerns that I encouraged him to send you an e-mail."

Larry did the right thing, and so did Russ. It is because of their actions that we became aware of the effect our decisions had on our franchisees. It was because of them that we had to make things right.

I called Debbie, our chief administrative officer, and Mike, who is now the president and CEO but was then our chief operating officer. I reminded them of the change to the Top Gun rules we had decided on and explained about Russ's e-mail and Larry's follow-up. We were all in full agreement that we needed to change the rules back to the original criteria. It wasn't long after that when we sent out an e-mail to the franchise network informing them of the change.

Wrong Foot, New Leaf

The keynote speech at Reunion that year was a success. But it was clear that we had earned some of the franchisees' respect as a result of understanding their perspective as well as the accountability we hold ourselves to for our own actions. And it was in part possible because our Code of Values gives everyone in our organization the opportunity to question our decisions and for us to make the situation right. We are serious about our values, and it has made us a better organization as a result.

Although I got off on the wrong foot with Russ, our timely response to his concerns and need for clarification allowed us to start over. He came to respect the Code of Values even more. In a separate discussion, he told us his newfound perspective.

"I think the Code of Values is great," he said. "We try to live by it as much as we can. We don't always do it, but it's like anything else in life. Life isn't perfect. You just have to keep working at it."

Clarification
Value Reflection

Have you ever neglected to ask a teacher,
a manager, or a role model for clarification when
you really needed it? If so, why?

Have you ever been given instructions on
something you didn't fully understand, but
instead of asking, you told yourself, "I'll figure it
out"? Would the results have turned out better if
you had asked for clarification the first time?

Is there something in your work, school, or home
life that you just "don't get"? If so, try asking
someone for clarification this week. As that
person responds, take note of how he or she
responds as well as how you are listening.
What did you learn?

Chapter Thirteen

Rumors: Weapons in the Workplace

*To retain those who are present, be loyal to those
who are absent.*

— *Stephen R. Covey*

We have all been both participants in and targets of rumors, hopefully less often in our later years than in our younger ones. We know the potential consequences that rumors we start or spread about people can have on them if they find out what we are saying about them. We know their pain, shame, sadness, and anger because we've experienced those feelings ourselves at one time or another when we've discovered what was being said behind our backs. There is no such thing as a harmless rumor; no matter how small the rumor might seem to those who spread it, the victim will inevitably feel hurt, wondering, "If it was just a 'small rumor,' why did they say it behind my back?"

For some, the workplace has become a war room, a proving ground for manipulation, covert strategy, and allied forces. The office war games sometimes continue even around the watercooler, where employees shoot the breeze or swap gossip. It's like maritime war, except the bombs and missiles take the form of words and insecurities.

The Workplace Bullying Epidemic

In many workplaces, there are "workplace bullies." These employees will use one or many of the tools in an adult bully's arsenal:

- Ignoring others

- Rude interruptions

- Negative criticism

- Humiliation

- Sarcastic jokes

- Harmful teasing

- Denigrating e-mails

- Rumors/gossip/slander

In one study, researchers found that 48 percent of employees have experienced or witnessed malicious gossip in the workplace. In another study, victims of workplace bullying described feeling like "slaves" or "prisoners" at work. This is a particularly astute observation—some victims report workplace bullying as being "like Chinese water torture."

Chinese Water Torture

Chinese water torture is a method first written about in the fifteenth century that involves strapping a victim down and slowly dripping very hot or very cold water in irregular intervals on an exposed body part, usually the forehead. The repeated dripping of hot or cold water on the forehead of the victim has been shown to drive torture victims to insanity by wearing them down little by little, drop by drop. Isn't the metaphor of workplace bullying as being "like Chinese water torture" strikingly appropriate? Studies have revealed that tactics used in bullying have a real and profound impact on its victims. Such impact includes:

- Decreased:
  - Job satisfaction
  - Self-esteem
  - Problem-solving ability
  - Productivity
  - Motivation

- Increased:
  - Stress
  - Anxiety
  - Depression
  - Stress-related health problems
  - Use of sick days
  - Fatigue and inability to fall asleep
  - Overall absenteeism
  - Likelihood of resigning

Of employees who experience workplace bullying, there is a 51 percent higher rate of absenteeism, a 45 percent higher rate of stress-related health problems, and a 25 percent resignation rate because of bullying. As a result, 89 percent of respondents in one survey reported that they wished their workplace had an anti-bullying policy and codes of conduct that address bullying issues. All of this certainly indicates that workplace bullying is a recipe for insanity.

The Impact of Bullying on Companies

It should come as no surprise that a negative impact on employees causes a negative impact on the company. The negative impacts of bullying that companies experience include:

- Difficulty sharing information and knowledge

- Difficulty establishing strong teams

- Increased risk of dysfunctional teams

- Difficulty improving organizational culture

- Increased employee resistance to change

- Increased misinformation and misunderstanding

- Decreased morale

- Decreased employee trust

- Decreased employee initiative

- Low quality of work output

- Increased absenteeism

- Higher employee turnover

- Difficulty attracting the "best and brightest"

- Bad press

- Loss of customer trust

- Decreased sales

- Decreased securities prices and earnings

- Loss of stockholder trust in the company and in management

This is no small matter! In fact, the issue of workplace bullying is far more prevalent than some might think: One study showed that 37 percent of the entire U.S. workforce reports being bullied on a regular basis. That amounts to 54 million Americans, which is the combined populations of Arizona, California, Nevada, Oregon, Utah, and Washington!

The "No Jerks" Rule

In 2001, Lars Dalgaard created SuccessFactors, a cloud-based employee performance management software company. SuccessFactors has enjoyed years of success and was at one point one of the world's fastest-growing software companies. It is also known for having a dramatically low employee turnover rate. The secret to the company's success?

"Employing no jerks."

That's right, the company strives never to hire "jerks." In fact, in founding the company, Dalgaard developed the company's "Rules of Engagement." One of the rules, number 14, is written as:

I will be a good person to work with—not territorial, not be a jerk. Our organization will consist only of people who absolutely love what we do, with a white-hot passion. We will have utmost respect for the individual in a collaborative, egalitarian, and meritocratic environment—no blind copying, no politics, no parochialism, no silos, no games—just being good!

Another company with a similar, albeit more informal, policy is Southwest Airlines. "People are hired and fired for attitude," says Herb Kelleher, the company's cofounder and former CEO. "One of our pilot applicants was very nasty to one of our receptionists, and we immediately rejected him. You can't treat people that way and be the kind of leader we want."

Have Integrity, Will Travel

When it comes down to it, deciding that you will not speak about people behind their backs in ways that you would not speak to their faces is all about integrity, honesty, respect, and trust. Successful workplaces take these values seriously. But no matter how serious a company is, no workplace is perfect, including The Dwyer Group. It's easy to get worked up on occasion and feel the need to "vent," but sometimes venting can be taken too far and can turn into bullying.

We all know the effect that gossip and other forms of bullying can have on people at work and at home, but what about our customers? How can we earn their respect? Their trust? Their loyalty?

Rumors
Value Reflection

Have you ever gotten enjoyment out of listening to gossip or a rumor about someone? Have you ever spread a rumor? Have you started one? For each one, articulate the reasons why.

What is the biggest rumor or gossip you have ever found out that people were saying about you? Were you surprised about who was spreading or starting the gossip or rumor? How did it make you feel?

Have you ever heard a rumor or gossip about one of your friends or family members? Did you stand up for your friend or family and/or tell the people spreading the rumor to stop? If not, why?

When does "venting" about people cross the line into gossiping or spreading rumors about them?

Customer Focus

Your most unhappy customers are your greatest source of learning.

- Bill Gates

Chapter Fourteen

Customer Loyalty

If you treat your employees right, they're happy and proud and partici-pate with respect to what they're doing. They manifest that attitude to your customers and your customers come back.

- Herb Kelleher, founder, Southwest Airlines

Darla slumps in her wheelchair, staring out the window. To her, the window is the frame of a living painting of a bright green-blue-gold world. She is the observer, the admirer on the other side in her stale, sterile, faded nursing home room. She watches the manic squirrels darting about and hears the clarion calls of songbirds. She sees other people's grandchildren, neatly dressed, disappear through the glass doors of the nursing home's entrance. She reflects on her childhood years and strains to remember what it felt like to get out of bed, young bones yearning to move and run and jump without pain and without the seriousness that stifles adults.

But the forceful, hacking cough-gasp-coughs of the tenant in the next room dissolve her memories behind the veil of reality. The death-encroaching sounds of her neighbor are a reminder of her doctor's recent words: "Darla, I need to let you know that the latest test results are not good."

She is blessed with the wisdom of decades come and gone—she knew that the moment people often dread was, for her, all too real and all too quickly approaching.

"How long do I have left, doctor?" she intoned, her voice a hoarse remnant of her lively, higher-pitched former self. The clock on the wall clicked steadily in the silence. The second hand seemed to drag. The doctor exhaled a burdened sigh.

"My best estimate is about four months, give or take. But it's really anybody's guess, Darla—it could be less but it could be more." His kindly eyes and solemn expression stand out in her mind. It's the same expression everyone seems to have these days when interacting with her. Their pity is a constant reminder of his words and has, of late, dampened her efforts at her remaining moments of joy. *Why go on?* she thinks. When she recently began refusing her treatments, the nurses never failed to plead with her. *What's the point?* she would ask herself. *What hope is there anymore?*

Through the window, the approach of a large, clean white truck with a trailer brings her back to the present. The truck parks and a small team in bright gold shirts and green hats hurry to their tasks. They begin scattering across the lawn, tending to their areas. One of the men rides a lawn mower along the edges of the property. The noisy drone of its motor advances and recedes slowly. The sound begins its gradual return, growing louder.

Finally, the man on the mower reappears. He looks up at her. When they make eye contact, he smiles widely and waves. She doesn't respond—she almost forgot that the world outside can sometimes see her inside. But before the team leaves, she can see him riding past once more. He looks at her and smiles again. She lifts her hand and slowly waves. He waves back.

The week has come and gone, like a wave. And, like a wave, a new week approaches, carrying mowing day with it. Darla asks her nurse to roll her to the window. It's another beautiful day outside. She waits for the truck. When it arrives, the team exits and busies themselves to rise to their tasks. The man sits atop the lawn mower, and as he rides past, he is looking at her, his smile even wider and his wave bigger. She smiles back this time and returns his wave. The day is brighter to her with a happy face in it.

Many weeks pass, the routine the same, the hope returning. Darla gets up the courage to ask the nurse to take her outside that afternoon for mowing day. She sits in front of her mirror, her few make-up items strewn on the table before her. She clutches her lipstick, her hand trembling as she lifts it to her lips. The lipstick is slightly askew on her thin lips. After applying her powder and eye shadow, she is rolled outside. This is the first day in many weeks that she has felt the warmth of the sun and the crisp cleanness of spring air.

The truck returns and the team works for several hours to properly manicure the landscape. When they are almost done, the man walks across the lawn, toward Darla. He smiles at her.

"Hello there," he says when he is a few yards away.

"Hello," Darla says, smiling.

He holds out his hand. She reaches out and grabs it gently, her hand trembling. "I'm Sam. What's your name?"

"My name is Darla, dear."

"Well, it's nice to finally meet you, 'Darla Dear.'" They share a laugh.

She sees the logo on his shirt and is finally able to read it: THE GROUNDS GUYS. "I just love your shirt," she says with a grin. "The colors are so bright and beautiful!"

Sam chuckles. "Oh, this old thing?" He brushes some of the grass trimmings off. "Well, it would be a shame if you didn't have one too. I get them for all my friends. So then I'll have to bring one for you next time, now, won't I?"

He called me his friend! "Oh, my," she says, "that would be just lovely! Thank you, Sam!"

"No need to thank me, Darla. I should thank you for always making my Wednesdays brighter and happier." He smiles. "Well, it's been my pleasure to be able to meet you finally. But it looks like my team is all wrapped up and ready for our next stop."

He holds out his hand once more. She grips it tighter, holding on to the moment with her new friend.

"I'll see you next week!" he reassures her. She lets go. They wave.

As the nurse wheels Darla back to her room, Darla turns her head and announces, "I've decided."

"What have you decided?" the nurse asks.

"I've decided I will start doing my treatments."

Spring becomes summer. Sam begins wheeling Darla around the facilities while they talk each week. Summer peaks and falls into autumn. It's the last mowing day for more than a season. Darla is in her gold The Grounds Guys T-shirt, waiting for their weekly post-mowing talk. Their conversation lasts longer than usual. They discuss family, Thanksgiving, Christmas. They exchange funny stories and her love of the Yankees. When the discussion comes to a close, he leans down and gives her a hug. She wraps her soft, bony arms around his neck and hugs back as tight as she can. They both hold back their tears.

Winter comes. Thanksgiving is served on paper plates. Christmas lights glow and tinsel sparkles on small plastic trees. Red and pink construction paper hearts stick to doors and purple cupids pose, dangling on string from between the ceiling tiles.

The snow melts. The rains come. Dead and wilted flora return with the life-giving breath of water and sunshine. Spring officially arrives. The moment Darla has anticipated for many months arrives when Sam walks up and holds his arms out to hug her. She is in her gold T-shirt and is overjoyed to see him. They embrace like old friends who have not been separated for more than a day. Sam resumes his ritual of wheeling Darla around the facilities while they pick up their weekly conversations where they left off.

Almost twelve months after first meeting Sam, Darla wakes up feeling ill. Days pass and her health declines. She is unable to come outside on mowing day, but she hears his lawnmower ride past her window several times. To her, it's the sound that a friend is close by.

In Darla's final few days, she makes her last wish known to her family.

"I want to be buried with my Bible, my Yankees cap, and my gold T-shirt that my friend Sam gave me."

More Than a Logo

One of our franchisees from The Grounds Guys e-mailed me a shorter version of this true story about one of his grounds-care technicians and that technician's friendship with Darla. In reading the story, I can see that for Darla the T-shirt was more than its color or logo; it was the tangible symbol of an important friendship with a man who just happened to be an employee of the local The Grounds Guys. And that's really the message of this book: The values a company embraces are not just another marketing tool, like a logo, but rather the mission statement for how a business treats and cares for the people who interact with or work in it. So, as you can imagine, when I first read this story, it gave me goose bumps.

Herb Kelleher once said, "You can buy all of the physical things. . . . You can't buy dedication, devotion, loyalty—the feeling you are participating in a crusade." A *crusade*. It calls to mind the idea of a band of people driven by a common mission, a common driving force, a common set of values. This is what any values-driven organization should represent. And when employees and customers respond to the call of the crusade, results can exceed expectations and change the paradigm of what it means to be a company. Perhaps we should call it what it is: the Caring Crusade.

The Flood

Memorial Day 1981. The pregnant clouds darken the city of Austin, Texas. Torrential rains free-fall and soak the grass, the cement, the buildings. Water rises, burying the roads and loosening the grip of tires.

The flooding gets to dangerously high levels. Cars are swept away. Buildings are no longer immune to the pressures of water. By the end of the day, Austin has sustained $100 million in damage in today's dollar value, and thirteen people have died in the flood.

The tragedy of the community is the sum of the tragedies of the lives within it. For the founders of Whole Foods, the tragedy is the destruction of their eight-month-old business. Tears fill their eyes as they look around at four hundred thousand dollars' worth of inventory and equipment soaked and scattered across the store. The start-up is still in its infancy—no insurance, no savings, no way to recover financially.

Renewed hope begins with the first few customers and neighbors who bring buckets and mops and a willingness to clean up the mess and start over. Hope continues over the coming weeks, as customers continue to come to the store to help clean up, day after day. For some reason, the community values Whole Foods too much to let it drown in water and bankruptcy.

"Why are you doing this?" one of the founders asks a customer.

"Whole Foods is really important to me. I'm not sure I would even want to live in Austin if Whole Foods wasn't here, if it ceased to exist. It has made a huge difference in my life."

Against Corporate Policy

Zaz Lamarr's mother was becoming more ill by the day. She tried everywhere to find shoes that would fit her mother, who had recently lost a lot of weight. After ordering several pairs from Zappos.com, she finally found two that fit. But the exhaustion of around-the-clock care for her mother kept the disheveled pile of oversize shoes in boxes stagnant.

Not long after Zaz found the fitting pairs after trying on multiple sizes, her mother passed away. In her grief, Zaz forgot all about the unreturned shoes. Zappos sent her an e-mail asking about the shoes, since they hadn't yet received them. She explained the situation to the customer support representative who had e-mailed her. The representative promptly replied to her e-mail, explaining that they were arranging to have UPS come to Zaz's house to pick up the shoes and return them. As Zaz would later find out, this was going against the company's policy.

But the customer support representative didn't stop at that. As Zaz explained it on her blog post titled "I Heart Zappos":

> *Yesterday, when I came home from town, a florist delivery man was just leaving. It was a beautiful arrangement in a basket with white lilies and roses and carnations. Big and lush and fragrant. I opened the card, and it was from Zappos. I burst into tears. I'm a sucker for kindness, and if that isn't one of the nicest things I've ever had happen to me, I don't know what is.*

The kindness Zappos showed to Zaz is not unusual for the company whose mission is to "deliver happiness." As a result, over 75 percent of Zappos customers are repeat buyers.

The Benefits of the Caring Crusade

What's hard to imagine isn't how companies such as Whole Foods and Zappos have become the successes they are, but rather how they couldn't have. But does it begin with customer service? If the customer is an internal one (i.e., an employee), then yes.

Gallup surveys many organizations throughout the country. One of the questions Gallup asks employees in its surveys is a true-or-false question: "Someone at work cares about me." What Gallup has found is that the companies in the lowest 25 percent of this response have a 22 percent higher employee turnover rate than companies in the highest 25 percent.

Another study finds that ethical companies who treat their employees right experience higher levels of employee loyalty, commitment, and efficiency. Furthermore, there is a direct correlation between employee morale and increased revenues. Think about it: When employees are happy and feel that someone at work cares about them, it improves the quality of the product or service, which translates to higher levels of customer loyalty. Customer loyalty equals increased revenues. In fact, every two percent increase in service quality equates to a one percent increase in revenues. A little kindness goes a long way.

But, as Darla showed us, the logos and the colors and the advertisements don't create a company's identity—values do. Our values and our kindness toward others cannot be forced—they come from a place within our hearts that is wholly authentic and transformed. Because of this, our values and our love are the foundation of our individual identities.

All of these studies point to one thing: The Caring Crusade starts in the workplace and in the home. It is from this point, and from a place of sympathy, that the Caring Crusade continues out into the world and transforms the lives of all those we meet. And it doesn't have to be a financial or time-consuming form of caring, either: To one lonely and dying elderly woman named Darla, caring is as simple as a genuinely kind smile from a man who mowed the lawn in the world outside her window.

Customer Loyalty
Value Reflection

How do you define a customer?

Whether you work or not, who are
your customers?

Have you ever done something selfless and
genuine for one of your customers?

Have you ever ignored or negatively treated one
of your customers? Why?

When was the last time you were negatively
treated as a customer? How did it make you feel?
Did you tell anyone about your experience?

When was the last time you were treated with
unexpected kindness as a customer? How did it
make you feel? Did you tell anyone about
your experience?

Chapter Fifteen

Understanding Needs

No person was ever rightly understood until they had been first regarded with a certain feeling, not of tolerance, but of sympathy.

- Thomas Carlyle, Scottish philosopher and writer,
1795-1881

Doug is crouched, tilting his head to look at the pipes under Mrs. Northguard's sink. He stands up and asks her, "Have you had any other issues with drains around the house?"

"Not that I've noticed," she says. She's rubbing the charm on her necklace, looking from side to side. She turns back to him. "Excuse me, I'm sorry." She leaves the kitchen and turns down the hallway. Doug hears several doors open and shut. A minute later, she returns and stops just outside the kitchen and sighs forcefully, looking around.

"Is everything okay, ma'am?"

Mrs. Northguard's lips are pressed together so tightly that they turn almost white. She crosses her arms. "I can't find my dog, Chow, anywhere," she says, voice quavering. She looks at him again and explains, "He's old and blind—I like knowing where he is at all times."

Doug sets his clipboard and pen down on her counter. "I'll help you look for him. Don't worry," he says, smiling kindly, "we'll find him."

They set off separately around the house. Doug starts with the living room, scanning the furniture and squatting to glance under the coffee table. He stands back up, placing his hands on his hips, craning his neck to look around for another room to review.

Mrs. Northguard screams, "Chow! No!"

Doug runs toward her screams. She is standing in the back-yard. He sees that her large, overweight dog is bobbing and swim-ming in the lake, a half-dozen yards out from the shore at the end of her yard.

"Chow! Come back!" she shouts. Doug's whistle pierces like a gunshot across the lake. The dog turns and begins to swim back toward the shore.

"Oh!" Mrs. Northguard whimpers. Her trembling hand is pressed helplessly against her forehead. The dog is nearly to the shore, ten feet out. Then, clearly exhausted, disoriented because of his blindness, he turns back out toward the heart of the lake and continues swimming. Mrs. Northguard becomes frantic.

"Chow! Stop! Come back!"

Doug whistles as loud as he can, but the dog doesn't respond.

"He never goes out that far!" she yelps. "He's too old and weak to swim back! Please, I don't know how to swim—you . . . you have to save him!"

She didn't even have to ask—Doug was already swiftly remov-ing his phone, wallet, and keys from his pockets. He drops them to the ground. He hops in place while he yanks his boots off.

Then, without hesitation, he runs.

He reaches the shallows, runs out several yards, and then launches into a jumping dive. The water is cold, but the adrenaline helps him swim as fast and powerfully as his body will allow. The dog seems to be swimming faster, farther than he is. Doug is in a race to catch up to him, to gain distance on the seemingly unsur-passable opponent that is Time.

Chow begins whining and panting. He is becoming fatigued and starts leaning to his side.

Doug is only a few feet away. The dog's paddling is becoming more uncoordinated and arrhythmic, his paws slapping at the water and splashing foamy droplets into chaotic arcs. Chow dips under the surface and back up in a frenzy.

"Chow! Come here!" Doug shouts between weighty breaths.

Trying to keep his nose above the surface, Chow begins tilting his head back. As the splashes become more frenzied, the dog's eyes flutter in the water. Chow stops paddling and plunges, disappearing. Doug hears Mrs. Northguard's distant screams.

He lunges forward and wraps his arm around the dog's torso, lifting it up above the surface. Chow blinks, inhales sharply, and looks at him with droopy eyes clouded by cataracts.

"Good boy," Doug says, "that's it."

Doug uses his free arm and his legs and his remaining might to propel them back to shore. Chow paddles lightly, helping Doug as much as he can to swim back.

They reach the shallows and Doug stands, lifting the ninety-pound dog in his arms and carrying him to Mrs. Northguard, who's in tears.

"Oh, my poor, poor baby!" she cries, "Oh, Chow!"

Doug sets the weary dog at her feet. She kneels down to hug Chow's neck. Doug bends over, hands buttressed against his knees, winded and worn. His shirt and pants, soaked, stick to his skin as he catches his breath. Water mixes with sweat and streams down his face in rivulets.

Mrs. Northguard looks up at Doug, crying. "Thank you! I just—I can't thank you enough!"

Doug stands up slowly. He swallows a gasp and smiles, chest heaving. "No need to thank me, ma'am." He bends back down, grabs the mouths of his boots, and lifts them off the ground. "I'm just glad I was here to help poor old Chow."

Selflessness and Humility

This story was told to me by Doug's boss, Vincent. Vincent is one of our Mr. Rooter franchise owners. During one of their morning meetings the day after Doug saved Chow, Doug only mentioned in passing that he'd had to jump in a lake the day before to save a dog. The team didn't think much of it except that the idea of Doug swimming in his uniform was humorous. It was later in the day that Vincent received a call from Mrs. Northguard, grateful and relieved as she retold the story of Doug's heroism the day before. As she spoke, Vincent was taken aback by Doug's humility and courage.

This story is not about Mr. Rooter. It's not about plumbing. It's about the character of a good man whom Vincent hired. It's about the selflessness of a man who put his customer's needs before his job. It's about the living example of our Code of Values that Doug is. He acted exactly in line with one of our values that day: *We live our Code of Values by making our best efforts to understand and appreciate the customer's needs in every situation.*

Service to Society

Bill George is the former CEO of Medtronic and a Harvard Business School professor. He once said, "We need new leadership: authentic leaders, people of the highest integrity, committed to building enduring organizations . . . leaders who have the courage to build companies to meet the needs of all their stakeholders, and who recognize the importance of their service to society."

I believe that individuals and businesses alike provide a service to society. In some cases, people and companies provide a disservice. In either case, the quality of our service is determined by one truth: Our minds don't lead people; our hearts and our values do.

No Limits on Safety

As members of an organization, it's easy to forget that "customers" means internal customers too. Employees or volunteers play a vital role in any type of organization. But they're not just "employees" or "volunteers" or "customers"; they are, above all, *people*. And people have a basic psychological and biological need for compassion, whether they are at home, school, or work.

Paul O'Neill understands this. He is the former CEO of Alcoa, an aluminum manufacturer. At the beginning of his tenure as CEO, in 1987, one of the first things he told plant managers was, "From now on, we're not going to budget for safety. As soon as anyone identifies anything that could get someone hurt, I want you to fix it and I will figure out how to pay for it." Then he flew across the country to meet with union leaders and hourly workers so he could tell them about his command to the plant managers. He gave the union leaders and workers his home phone number and said, "And if they don't do what I said, I want you to call me."

He was serious about his statements too; he wasn't just reciting them to "look the part" of a caring CEO. He gathered a small group of graduates from Carnegie Mellon University and asked them to create a real-time system to report safety issues. One of his requirements was that the reports were to include the names of those who got injured. Although the legal counsel from Alcoa was uncomfortable with this move, he later explained his reasoning: "One of the things I've learned is if you're managing numbers, it feels a lot different than if you're dealing with individuals, human lives and injuries to people. So if somebody got hurt, I didn't want to penalize them by calling their name out. But I wanted their co-workers to know, 'My friend got hurt. This is another human being. This is not about OSHA recordable rates or something—this is about individual human beings who are part of our family.'"

His philosophy on safety is an extension of his philosophy on what makes an organization great. Greatness, to him, is when every person within the company can answer yes, without hesitation, to all three of these questions:

1. Can I say every day I am treated with dignity and respect by everyone I encounter without respect to my pay grade, or my title, or my race, or ethnicity or religious beliefs or gender?

2. Am I given the things I need—education, training, tools, encouragement—so I can make a contribution to this organization that gives meaning to my life?

3. Am I recognized for what I do by someone I care about?

His philosophy has led Alcoa to attain his definition of greatness. In fact, during his 13 years as CEO, the company went from 1.86 lost workdays per 100 workers to 0.2.

Empathetic Leaders

Empathy is the emotional capability to put oneself in the shoes of others. It's the reason we cry at other people's tragedies, wince at the sight of someone getting hurt, or smile when children laugh. As famous psychologist Dr. Daniel Goleman, the author of *Emotional Intelligence*, explains it: "Empathetic people are superb at recognizing and meeting the needs of clients, customers, or subordinates. They seem approachable, wanting to hear what people have to say. They listen carefully, picking up on what people are truly concerned about, and respond on the mark."

As a result of their character, empathetic leaders are better at communicating with and inspiring employees. Because of this, employees of empathetic leaders tend to stay longer with, and work harder for, their companies. Gallup's poll of more than two million employees across seven hundred companies in the U.S. revealed that employees' productivity is correlated with the quality of their relationship with their supervisor.

Stronger relationships tend to correlate with a higher degree of shared values. These shared values promote understanding with other members of society, and are a guide to people for finding fulfillment of basic needs. One study found that work environments that have a higher likelihood of fulfilling one's needs, personal characteristics, and values report higher rates of satisfaction among employees. But besides love, caring, and empathy, there is one other basic need that is too often forgotten by today's companies: our basic human need to have fun.

Understanding Needs
Value Reflection

Have you ever needed something from someone
at a time that happened to be difficult for him or
her? Did you ask him or her for what you needed
anyway? If so, why? If not, why not?

Have you ever wanted something that someone
else needed more? Who was that person? Did you
let him or her have it? If so, why?
If not, why not?

What do you think are every person's basic needs
in life? Do you know anyone who is lacking the
means to fulfill one of those needs? Think of a
way you can help meet his or her need this week.

Having Fun

All animals, except man, know that the principal business of life is to enjoy it.

- Samuel Butler

Chapter Sixteen

Fun Times

People rarely succeed unless they have fun in what they are doing.

- Dale Carnegie

"Welcome to Southwest Airlines flight 245 to Tampa." The flight attendant's voice sounds slightly metallic over the intercom as she speaks, holding the handheld speaker a little too close to her mouth.

"To operate your seat belt, insert the metal tab into the buckle, and pull tight. It works just like every other seat belt, and if you don't know how to operate one, you probably shouldn't be out in public unsupervised."

A chorus of giggles and laughs scatters across the plane as they listen to the flight attendant begin her comedic take on otherwise redundant instructional dialogue.

"In the event of a sudden loss of cabin pressure, masks will descend from the ceiling. Stop screaming, grab the mask, and pull it over your face. If you have a small child traveling with you, secure your mask before assisting with theirs. If you are traveling with more than one small child, decide now which one is your favorite."

The passengers laugh even louder. One lady even guffaws from the midsection of the plane. The flight attendant's name is Yvonne LeMaster and she enjoys making people's flights—and her job— fun.

"If you smoke in the lavatory, the FAA will fine you two thousand dollars." Yvonne pauses a beat. "And at *those* prices, you might as well fly Delta!"

But Yvonne is not the only flight attendant at Southwest Airlines who enjoys having fun on the job. On another flight, the attendant has a different version of this joke. "Ladies and gentlemen, if you wish to smoke, the smoking section on this airplane is on the wing and if you can light 'em, you can smoke 'em."

In fact, most of the flight attendants and pilots at Southwest make it their mission to have fun and make it fun for customers. It's even a part of the company's core values:

Fun-LUVing Attitude

- Have FUN

- Don't take yourself too seriously

- Maintain perspective

- Celebrate successes

- Enjoy your work

- Be a passionate Teamplayer

It's a part of the company's recruitment process to ask applicants during a job interview, "Have you ever used humor to solve a workplace problem?" But what is the workplace problem that flight attendants and pilots face? It's a customer problem, one that famous actor and director Orson Welles once pointed out: "There are only two emotions on a plane: boredom and terror."

By having unassigned seating, low fares, and lighthearted and witty service, Southwest Airlines has won a cult following the world over ever since Herb Kelleher started the company in 1971.

"Ladies and gentlemen," Yvonne continues, "please put your faces against the windows on the left side of the plane, toward the terminal, so that our competitors can see what a full flight looks like."

It's not just one-liners that flight attendants turn to; the crew on many flights have been known to throw in-flight snacks for passengers to catch. Others dance, sing, and—yes—even rap. Some of them are also actors and standup comedians on the side. For Southwest, life is too short to take too seriously. Their philosophy of fun has brought joy not just to the lives of customers, but to the lives of the employees. This is no industry secret either: In 2013, the company received 100,682 résumés but hired only 1,521 people, bringing the total to 44,831 employees. Additionally, 2,830 of those employees have spouses who work for Southwest.

While the plane taxis around the tarmac on a busy day, the wait for takeoff seems longer than usual. To defuse the frustration of waiting, Yvonne gets on the intercom and remarks, "Ladies and gentlemen, this is how we keep our fares so low. We drive halfway, fly the rest." The passengers laugh and begin to see the humor in a frustrating situation that befalls many a flight.

Goleman summarizes academic research on the subject of workplace humor. He reports findings showing that jokes and laughter at work help foster creativity, trust, and communication among employees. He also reports that light, friendly banter during negotiations increases the chances that the conceding party will loosen their financial requirements.

"Can I have your attention, ladies and gentlemen. We have a special guest with us up front today. It's his eightieth birthday today and this is his *first flight*. Let's everyone give him a big round of applause!" Yvonne smiles cheerfully and claps her hands too. She gets back on the intercom. "You know, it'd be even nicer if, on your way out, you just stick your head in the cockpit and wish our pilot a happy birthday." The passengers laugh wildly—they didn't see that one coming.

Some business executives have heard that having fun at work is better for the business and employees, but they hesitate to adjust their culture because they aren't sure how much better it really would be. Aside from making the lives of people at work better, fun and humor help improve the positive perception that people have of their leaders. In fact, Goleman also finds that in surveys taken by employees, leaders who were rated as "outstanding" made, on average, three times the number of witty remarks as "average" leaders.

The plane has completed most of its descent and is nearly to the runway. The ground rises; the plane tilts back. The impact of the landing makes the plane bounce in a jerking motion, and the pilot maneuvers the wings delicately, causing the plane and passengers to tilt side to side until the craft is stable and at a drivable speed. Yvonne knows that landings are uncomfortable for nervous flyers. She gets on the intercom.

"That was quite a bump and I know what y'all are thinking. I'm here to tell you it wasn't the airline's fault, it wasn't the pilot's fault, it wasn't the flight attendant's fault. It was the asphalt!" People chuckle, still unwinding from the jarring touchdown. Then, the pilot has his turn.

"Ladies and gentlemen, we are pleased to have some of the best flight attendants in the industry. Unfortunately, none of them are on this flight." Everyone, even Yvonne, lets loose with laughter.

Even in difficult, high-tension, or high-pressure situations that some flyers face on occasion, Southwest's humor is so effective and well received precisely because of the nature of positive emotions: They are contagious. One Yale University study discovered that emotions such as cheerfulness and kindness spread throughout offices quicker than irritability and gloominess. Other studies show that smiles are actually contagious—when you smile at people, you transmit your happiness to them.

The "happiness infection" is not a disease to be feared, but a "bug" to catch, one that millions of Southwest customers have caught and enjoyed. It has led the company to total operating revenues of $17.7 billion in 2013, as well as dozens of awards over the years. These awards from prestigious publications and organizations are in categories such as Most Admired Company in the World (ninth place) in *Fortune* magazine, Number One in Customer Service in 2013 Airline Quality Rating, 2012 Eco-Pioneer of the Year by Air Transport World, and one of the Best Places to Work in 2014 from the Glassdoor Employees' Choice Awards.

After the plane arrives at the gate, Yvonne thanks the passengers and then reminds everyone, "As you exit the plane, make sure to gather all of your belongings. Anything left behind will be distributed evenly among the flight attendants. Please do not leave children or spouses." One for the road. People smile and laugh as they travel to their destination, some of them even cheerfully recalling some of their favorite zingers. The Southwest "happiness infection" has been released into the world, making small differences in the days of travelers. And these customers will return.

It's truths like these that are evidenced by the sounds of joy people make when employees enjoy their job. Happy employees make for happy customers; both of them make for happy lives. At the end of the day, though, the difference is made by leaders. This includes having fun in the process: Southwest Airlines has also been given recognition as one of the 2014 Best Companies for Leaders by the Chief Executive Group.

But having fun in the process can mean different things to different people and different leaders. Joking, playing games, and holding office parties aren't the only ways to have fun; volunteering or fundraising combines the values of fun and love. Mr. Electric discovered this truth when brainstorming creative ways to raise awareness about Ronald McDonald House Charities. The company ended up enlisting the help of Martin Bros. Bikes in Duncanville, Texas to build a Mr. Electric custom-made motorcycle as a prize in a fund-raising sweepstakes giveaway.

Other people consider "having fun" to mean the joy of bringing happiness to others. One of the things I enjoy most about my job is helping people achieve success in their lives and careers. It's why I love franchising so much! At The Dwyer Group, we have been very fortunate to enjoy the kind of growth that few companies have achieved. In 2014, we were reacquired by The Riverside Group, a private equity firm who shares our values. During the negotiation stage, I asked our private equity firm at the time, TZP Group, for certain terms to the agreement. TZP wasn't able to agree to everything, but they were extremely supportive of one of the terms that I was most adamant about: a $1 million bonus for our employees. The Dwyer Group would not have been so successful without the dedication and hard work of our employees and we wanted to find a fun way to say, "Thank you."

To be able to stand up and announce the bonus to all of the associates at the company, and to see the expressions of surprise and unexpected joy, is one of the most fun things about being a leader of our company. The executive team gained the same immense pleasure from surprising the employees that my family did when they provided a similar bonus in 2003 when The Dwyer Group went from public to private.

Big business isn't just about the success of the owners, it's about the success of the team; where we go, we go together. Why not have fun in the process?

Whether at work, at school, or at home, our values—kindness, understanding, accountability, honesty, fun, and love—are ingrained in our choices, which define our actions. And if we really stop and think about it, isn't action what truly makes the difference?

Having Fun
Value Reflection

What do you like to do for fun?

What is your favorite game? Movie?
TV show? Book?

Whom do you enjoy spending time
"decompressing" with?

What do you do with that person that allows
you to decompress?

Plan a Decompress Night with your family and/or
friends that involves an activity everyone enjoys.
Ask each of them what they most like
to do for fun.

Does your workplace or school ever do anything
you consider to be fun? Do you and your
coworkers ever do non-work-related
activities outside of work?

Action

The actions of men are the best interpreters of their thoughts.

- John Locke

Chapter Seventeen

How to Incorporate Your Values

Make sure you know what you really believe in, what you live and die by. And be clear on the mission of your life and the values you want to have guide it.

- John Pepper, former CEO, Proctor & Gamble

What if the sun could illuminate the depths of our hearts the way it does our skin? What if others could see the light glowing from within you, showing them what lies past the surface? What if the person in your life you most respect asked you, "Do you strive to align your thoughts, emotions, and actions with your personal values?" What would you say? What do you think other people would say?

Be honest. Be *brutally* honest—the kind of honesty that makes you wince in fearful anticipation, as if you're about to tear a bandage off your skin. There is nowhere else to start but from the truth. Maybe the truth is that you want to, but don't know where to begin. Maybe you didn't know until now how much of a difference values make. Or maybe you've never thought about what your values really are or how important they are to you. There are no wrong or bad answers; there are only two paths: action, or inaction.

This chapter is written for those of you who want to take action.

"Values are not trendy items that are to be casually traded in."

This quote by Ellen Goodman—journalist, women's rights activist, and Pulitzer Prize winner—perfectly sums up the anxiety felt in writing a book on the subject of values. This book is not intended to be read as the next trendy business book or self-help fad. Values are integral to the happiness of every individual and the success of our lives, relationships, and businesses. Aside from all of these benefits, the central point is this: Values guide us to make the *right* choices.

Brandon, who worked at our Aire Serv corporate office at the time, is a man of great integrity. In 2013, I received an e-mail from Ms. Washington, a local Waco resident, who was moved by Brandon's actions when she was out shopping one night. *Dear Dina*, the e-mail began:

> *A few days ago, I was in Kohl's here in Waco and a handsome man was standing in front of me with a Dwyer Group shirt on. As we were both waiting in line I noticed that he had only a receipt in his hand. When it was his turn to be waited on he asked to speak to the manager, and conveniently the man behind the counter was the store manager. What happened next I must say brings absolute JOY to my heart.*
>
> *Brandon proceeded to tell the manager that he and his wife had been in the store the night before and purchased some items; however, he had not been charged for them all. He went further in explaining that last night he even made the young lady check and recheck to make sure that she had gotten everything. Now Brandon explained that he was absolutely certain that she had made a mistake, but he didn't want to insult her. Therefore, he knew he would simply return today.*

The store manager, I, and everyone in line behind me could not believe what had just happened. Nonetheless, Brandon went through the receipt with the manager and pointed out the missing item. The store manager left to retrieve the item to scan for the correction. As he left, I chatted with Brandon, and I told him I knew the Dwyers slightly and it was a great company and so on. When the manager returned, he scanned the item, thanked Brandon repeatedly, and told him he would give him a 25 percent discount for his honesty.

As he swiped his card, I leaned forward and told him his honesty had just cost him a hundred dollars! Brandon smiled and winked, and said, I quote, "No ma'am, that money was never mine, so my honesty just got me a twenty-five percent discount."

When Brandon left, the store manager shook his head and said, "If the world were filled with more people like him, we would be much better off."

I couldn't agree more.

Although I already knew Brandon as a man who lives by the Code of Values, like Ms. Washington I was extremely impressed by the high level of integrity he exhibited. She concluded her e-mail with the following statement:

It's not what you do when everyone is watching that makes integrity; it's who you are when no one is around.

Her closing line is an echo of Goodman's quote: Values are not trendy items; they're fundamental choices. Brandon didn't make the choice he made *because* The Dwyer Group has a written Code of Values; he made the choice he made *because* he, like the rest of the employees at our company, embodies those values at work and at home.

Research shows that simply having a written set of values is not enough to change ethical behavior in organizations; ethics should be entrenched in every aspect of the company's work life and decisions. This is why it is important to have people like Brandon in your company and in your life. Furthermore, other research shows that in order to influence ethical behavior in a company, a leader actually has to exhibit those ethical behaviors.

Investing in Values

In 1993, Don Dwyer led The Dwyer Group to become a publicly traded company on NASDAQ: DWYR, our ticker symbol. It was a new era for us. But like all eras, it faded as a new one came into focus.

September 11, 2001, hit and the economy changed course. We began to entertain the idea of going private again. We met with a private equity firm, The Riverside Company, and although our numbers guided many of the discussions, I was most interested in preserving one thing: our Code of Values. In the world of private equity, discussing shared values is far down the list of talking points. That's why I was surprised to hear how important values were to them and that they wanted to ensure we continued to preserve our Code of Values.

In 2003, The Riverside Company purchased The Dwyer Group for $6.70 per share—more than 50 percent premium on the then-current stock price. Why were they so set on acquiring a company whose values were at the forefront of the business? Not long ago, I e-mailed Riverside's co-CEO, Stewart Kohl, on this subject. He wrote back to me:

It's our strong belief that higher values lead to higher value. A few years ago we started to track "ESG+V" for all of our acquisitions. It's right at the bottom of the front page of our investment committee memos and stands for Environmental, Social, Governance, and Values. Our goal is to achieve higher grades [on this scale] when we sell a company than when we bought it.

Fraud has been the most consistent contributor to our losses over the past 25 years. People doing bad things is the biggest risk in our business. So we know for a fact that bad values leads to bad outcomes.

I also heard from Béla Szigethy, founder and co-CEO of The Riverside Company, and he told me:

Twenty-six years ago when I founded The Riverside Company I decided to lead with some simple rules—the Golden Rule, and leaving great references in our wake. Private equity—or as our industry was known in those days, LBOs (leveraged buyouts)—was not known for its values. I figured it might cost me a few points of return, but I'd still make a decent living and I'd be happy to see myself in the mirror shaving each morning.

Now, 350 acquisitions later, I've been delighted to find out that living with principles has been one of the keys to our success. It is nice to know that our modern, hypercompetitive world works in this way and that you are rewarded BOTH psychically and financially for good values. And we've seen this reinforced in the performance of the companies in which we invest . . . and specifically we can see how companies that fall short on values often disappoint as investments.

It is no surprise, then, that in 2010 The Riverside Company sold The Dwyer Group to TZP Group for a high rate of return. My concern in being sold to another company was that we would be hard-pressed to find a private equity firm with as strong a stance on values as The Riverside Company. But my concerns were quickly put to rest when TZP Group pulled me and my CFO, Tom Buckley, aside less than three months after acquiring our company. They showed us a piece of paper. On it was written a set of values. "Tell us if you believe we are living these values," Sam Katz, the managing partner of TZP Group, said to us. We were taken aback and touched by the example that they said The Dwyer Group had set for them.

I firmly believe that our Code of Values has led us to the success we've seen today. It is evidenced by the employees we have who lead by example, by the franchisees in the field who spread the benefit of their values to their customers, and by the continued high return on investments private equity firms have with our company.

After our sale to TZP, I half-jokingly asked The Riverside Company when they would be buying us again. I say "half-jokingly" because while I would have loved to rejoin our partnership with them, reacquisition of a former investment by a private equity firm is extremely rare, *especially* since TZP Group wasn't yet ready to put The Dwyer Group back on the market. This passing statement snowballed into a reality in August 2014, when Riverside sought us out again and acquired our company for a second time by paying TZP Group's full asking price!

Independent research has backed up Béla's and Stewart's claims that values-based companies outperform non-values-based companies. One study shows that organizations with higher financial and nonfinancial performance than other companies have management that "treats people with respect, creates individual relationships with employees, encourages trust in others, treats people fairly, communicate values, have and enforce accountability, are perceived as credible and consistent, and have a strong sense of ethics."

When companies employ and set an example of a written set of values, they should expect to see an increase in employee participation, which increases employee satisfaction, engagement, and productivity. Therefore, managers will not feel as compelled to watch every move their employees make. In other words, actually living and reinforcing a written set of values increases the trust, happiness, and profitability of companies. This then increases people's freedom and companies' profits, which decreases people's financial and psychological needs, thereby increasing the happiness levels of entire societies.

How, then, does a company, a family, or an individual go about developing a written set of values?

Creating Your Written Values

I think most people are surprised to find how simple developing their own set of written values can be. In fact, the simplicity of it is by design—the simpler the process, the more successful the outcome is likely to be. However, the fact that it is simple doesn't mean that it is *quick*. Creating your values is something that should be done thoughtfully and with heart. After all, you are expressing in written form, after near-meditative consideration, the core of your being and beliefs as an individual or an organization. (No pressure!)

The process of developing your values has only four steps:

- Knowing and understanding your values

- Regularly sharing your values and aligning yourself with people who embody them

- Systemization and internalization of your values

- Measuring your performance with values

Whether you are part of an organization, the founder of a small business, entry-level, an executive, a parent, a doctor, a lawyer, or a student, you are a leader and a good person. That means the process of developing your own written values applies to you and can make a difference in your life.

1. Knowing and Understanding Your Values

Before you decide how to write your values, you have to know what they are. You also have to understand what each value really means, beyond the basic definition. In other words:

You have to get clarity about your personal values.

If you are developing your written values as a member of a team within an organization, you should be sure to include key leaders and try to keep the number of people involved in this first step to a small group. This might sound like a contradictory statement. (Shouldn't everyone be a part of developing the company's written values?) But in fact, the intent of a set of written values is to live them. In order to ensure the organization maintains these values indefinitely, the leaders at the top have to lead by values that they feel they can truly embrace. This is because:

You have to genuinely know yourself before you can lead with strong values.

So what values matter to you? Where do you start? Whether it was in your workplace, at school, at church, or at home, think about times someone has really made a difference in your day. Think about times when someone has made your day worse. What are some things you have felt guilty for? What are some things you have done that have really made a difference in someone's life? For example, you might write down, *A coworker forgot to finish her part of a recent project and it caused the entire team to have to work overtime to complete the project by the deadline.*

While you build a list of these scenarios—either by yourself, as a family, or with a team—you might find that you instinctively know what it was about those situations and actions that resonated with you. This might lead back to a particular value such as honesty, or understanding others' perspectives. In the example of the coworker who didn't finish her task in the project, she had committed to an agreement she couldn't keep. Therefore, the value could be simplified in a short statement such as, *Make only agreements we are able to keep.* This could be distilled further as, *Keep commitments.*

In other cases, the values may be harder to identify, but once you've developed the list of scenarios, spend some time thinking deeply about what it was that made an impact—positive or negative—on your day or your life. If after a few days you're still stumped, you can also share your list with friends, family, or coworkers and see if they can identify the underlying value. The bottom line is, there's no rush, no deadline. Take your time—this first step is crucial.

By the end of this process, you should have identified the core values that mean the most to you as an individual or as a group. When you have these core values, it's time to write them in an easy-to-remember format. Many people or companies use acronyms. Others simply have a list of value statements. Some are long; others are short. There's no right or wrong format, but try to remember that whatever format you do choose, it should be something that is possible to memorize and easy enough to say. For example, while The Dwyer Group's Code of Values is in the format of "We live our Code of Values by . . ." followed by each value statement, I've seen many companies use an acronym. A fictional example might be:

S.M.A.R.T.
Speaking honestly
Making our best efforts in all we do
Acknowledging the perspectives of others
Responding in a timely fashion
Treating others with respect

Once you and your team (if you are doing this as a group) have decided on your core written values, share them with a select few people outside your team. Ask them if they share those values and if they think your company as a whole lives up to them. Which values do they think should be added? Which do they think your company could work on? Which ones do they think your company does well? If you're doing this as an individual or a family, ask a select few other friends or family members the same questions as they apply to your situation.

Before sharing your final written values with others outside this group, there is one final task in this step:

You must make the commitment to live these values.

Arguably, for many people this is the hardest part of all these steps. But that is a sign that it is the most important part. Until we, as leaders, make a commitment to change by personally demonstrating these values, no one will follow our lead. This is difficult for many leaders, especially those in more visible positions—such as executives or parents—because we know that we are human, and we know we will mess up from time to time. We don't want to be vulnerable to our mistakes, but mistakes are an opportunity to show that we are willing to own up to our shortcomings and make them right. Doing this exhibits its own values, such as honesty, responsibility, treating others as we would like to be treated, responding in a timely fashion, acknowledging everyone as right from their own perspective. The list could go on!

If and when you do make a mistake, however, it's important not to try to cover it up. It's far easier to destroy a reputation than to build one. If you want your reputation to be based on the values you believe in, own up to all of your actions, even the mistakes.

2. Regularly Sharing Your Values

After everyone involved in developing the written values has agreed upon the final draft and has made the commitment to live those values, it's time to share the written statement with other stakeholders. If you have written it as an individual or as a family, share it with other family members, friends, or mentors. If you have written it as a group within an organization or company, share it with the remaining members of the company. It is an exciting time! Set up a company-wide meeting and "unveil" the new written statement of values. Or order business cards with the values printed on them to make it easy to carry them in a wallet or purse or to share them at a moment's notice.

As you share these values, you might begin to notice some people are ecstatic that your values align with theirs. Others might find it new or odd that you have a written statement of values. There may even be some who share very few of your values and will find it difficult to keep a commitment to live those values. That's okay. But the key is this:

Coworkers, customers, friends, family, significant others, mentors—
anyone who joins in the commitment to live up to your values should
believe in *those values.*

This is why the brands at The Dwyer Group only award our franchises to people who we feel align with those values and who are willing to make the commitment to live those values. Not everyone will align with your values statement at first, but over time, your company—or your circle of friends, as the case may be—will begin to attract more people who identify with your values just because of the fact that you have begun living them.

3. Systemization and Internalization of Your Values

The Dwyer Group is in the business of systemization. I believe this is part of why we have been so successful at implementing our commitment to our values. Why? A franchise is a proven business system that is designed to be duplicated. It is in the process of systemization that we have found what makes our Code of Values stick: internalization. At The Dwyer Group, in meetings of three or more people, we take turns reciting each value from the Code of Values. At first, this might seem awkward or strange, but many skeptics have been turned into believers of this process because:

The more you recite your values, the more aware you are of those values in every situation, and the more you internalize and solidify the meaning of each value.

New employees find that we are serious about making our decisions based on these values. Upon discovering this, the act of reciting these values at meetings doesn't seem so strange! Whether at work or with your family, for these reasons it is a good idea to regularly read aloud your written statement of values and to think about how they apply to each situation.

As mentioned previously, committing to the values can be the hardest part for many people. We must remember that we will always make mistakes, and we will always need to improve how we live out our values. But with help, persistence, and patience, we will always get there. At The Dwyer Group, when we first unveiled the new Code of Values, we asked our employees to keep the executive team accountable. For the first 90 days, we invited our employees to literally "beep" out loud at us when they noticed any of us breaking one of the values. They didn't state which value they thought we were breaking; they just beeped. This not only had humorous effects, but it was extremely successful, for two reasons:

1. When executives were beeped at, they had to think about which value they had just violated, without any help from other people.

2. The employees took advantage of this Beep Game, as it came to be called, which actually had the effect of getting them to internalize which values we, as a company, had committed to. So in the process, they learned our Code of Values!

Many employees still play the Beep Game to this day. But since everyone is accountable for following the Code of Values now, everyone has the potential to be beeped, not just the executive team.

In the beginning, it's essential to do one thing right: *Ask* people, don't *force* them, to live the new values. If people feel forced to make a commitment, they won't internally make that commitment. Whether your new written statement is for a company, a family, a classroom, or for you, invite others to join with you, but don't expect everyone to say yes. Instead, let skeptics see why and how those values are important when, as a leader, you put them into action.

4. Measuring Your Performance with Values

Now that you've systemized and begun to internalize your written values, are you living up to your commitment? In making that commitment, you also committed to accept opportunities for improvement. But as individuals, we are inherently subjective and don't always see our mistakes the way others do. That's why it is important to measure how you are performing at living up to those values.

At The Dwyer Group, our brands regularly ask their franchisees every year through a survey to tell us how we have been doing. In the survey, they rate our company on each of our values and suggest areas for improvement. Our annual supervisor surveys operate in the same way: Through a survey, we ask our employees to rate how well their supervisor sets an example for each of the values. But this isn't just an obligatory "going through the motions" thing—we *use* this feedback as a mirror to spot our weaknesses. These weaknesses then become our new areas of improvement.

As a company, a classroom, a church, or an individual, for your situation measuring your performance might be as simple as choosing one value a month and publicly making a commitment to work on it. Then, you could revisit that value the next month with your employees, students, or friends and family and ask for their perspective on how well you did at improving it.

There are so many possibilities for how you could write, share, memorize, internalize, and measure your written values. This is because values are not limiting, as some might think; they are freeing. Why?

When we know where we want to be, we know where to go. When we know who we want to be, we know what to do.

Where We Go from Here

Why should we, as individuals or as a business, write our own set of values? Where do written values play a role in our lives? They remind us of the kinds of choices we want to make and the kind of people we want to be. When we identify our values, we discover a deeper part of ourselves that makes us who we are. When we write those values down and remind ourselves of them daily, we integrate that deeper part of ourselves into the forefront of our decisions and relationships. There are few things in today's world that offer an opportunity for such profound self-discovery!

Who we are and what we choose to do changes lives—no exceptions. Every good deed that was ever done was based on at least one value. Gandhi, Mother Teresa, Martin Luther King, Jesus. Patrick, Sam, Doug, Brandon. Whether we change lives all at once or one at a time, knowing our values and letting those values guide our actions means there is one thing we can all do:

We can change the world.

Epilogue

The values by which we are to survive are not rules for just and unjust conduct, but are those deeper illuminations in whose light justice and injustice, good and evil, means and ends are seen in fearful sharpness of outline.

- Jacob Bronowski, mathematician, inventor, and poet, 1908-1974

Lisa hesitates. She begins to reach for the pen that Ben handed her. *None of this makes any sense*, she thinks. *The values seemed so clear and good!* She stops and looks at him.

"Ben, I have to ask: Someone told me that Enron is not really serious about the Code of Ethics. Is that true?"

Ben laughs. "Let me put it this way: As long as you're making the company money, we're not going to stand in your way."

A moment of silence passes. Lisa smiles politely. "Thanks for the opportunity, Ben, but I can't take this job." Ben furrows his brow and scoffs.

As she turns to leave, she doesn't yet know that months later she will see these same offices all over the news. She doesn't yet know that Enron's bankruptcy of $63.4 billion will make it one of the largest corporate bankruptcies in history. Or that Jeffrey Skilling, Kenneth Lay, and Andrew Fastow will soon become the new faces of white-collar crime. She doesn't yet know that she will see these things on the news and think: *Happiness is more valuable than that.*

Appendix: List of Suggested Values

Below is a list of commonly-held values that you can use as a starting point when developing your personal or company code of values. Review each one with care, reflecting on which values strike a chord with you. Of those values, what are some situations that stand out in your mind in which those values were apparent (or absent)?

Adaptability
Achievement
Accountability
Advancement
Adventure
Attentiveness
Authority
Balance: (work
    home)
Being the best
Belonging
Breathing space
Caring
Caution
Challenge
Collegiality
Comfort
Commitment
Communication
Community
Compassion
Competition

Confidence
Contribution
Control
Cooperation
Creativity
Customer satisfaction
Dignity
Discontent
Discretionary time
Diversity
Empathy
Energy
Enthusiasm
Entrepreneurship
Environmental
    awareness
Ethics
Fairness
Faith
Family/Friends
Focus

Forgiveness
Friendship
Harmony
Honesty
Humor/Fun
Improvement
Independence
Influence
Information
Initiative
Innovation
Integrity
Intelligence
Involvement
Knowledge
Leadership
Learning, Formal
Learning, Informal
Listening
Location
Long-Term view
Love

Loyalty
Making a difference
Meetings
Money
Opportunities
Organizational
    growth
Partnering
Peace
Positive spirit
Power
Prestige
Profit
Productivity
Purpose
Quality
Recognition
Relationships
Relaxation
Reliability
Resilience
Respect/Valuing
Responsibility
Results
Reverence
Risk-Taking
Safety
Service
Socializing
Spirituality

Stamina
Status
Success
Teamwork
Territory
Tolerance
Tradition
Trust
Unity
Vacations
Variety
Vision
Wealth
Wisdom

List used with permission of Robert K. Cooper, Ph.D.
CooperStrategic.com

Endnotes

Chapter One

The company's Code of Ethics: McLean, B., & Elkind, P. (2003). The smartest guys in the room: The amazing rise and scandalous fall of Enron. New York: Penguin.

all of them are true: Callahan, D. (2004). The cheating culture: Why more Americans are doing wrong to get ahead. Orlando, FL: Harcourt.

"It is the government's job to step in if a product is dangerous.": Fusaro, P. C., & Miller, R. M. (2002). What went wrong at Enron: Everyone's guide to the largest bankruptcy in U.S. history. Hoboken, NJ: John Wiley & Sons.

"keep making us millions.": McLean & Elkind (2003).

large personal and company gains: Sims, R. R., & Brinkmann, J. (2003). Enron ethics (or: Culture matters more than codes). Journal of Business Ethics, 45(3), 243–256.

"I lost my moral compass and I did many things I regret.": Pasha, S. (2006, March 9). Enron trial: Defense skewers Fastow on the stand. CNNMoney.com. Retrieved from http://money.cnn.com/2006/03/08/news/newsmakers/enron/index.htm

book a free flight anytime in the future: Huettel, S. (2007, February 20). JetBlue issues fliers bill of rights. Tampa Bay Times. Retrieved from http://www.sptimes.com/2007/02/20/Business/Jet_Blue_issues_flier.shtml

avoid laying off or cutting the pay of any employees: Rhoades, A. (2011). Built on values: Creating an enviable culture that outperforms the competition. San Francisco: Jossey-Bass.

optional pay-period donation: Ibid.

with employees throughout the organization: Ibid.

share their tears: Stallard, M. L. (2011, July 27). The heart of Starbucks' CEO. Michaelleestallard.com. Retrieved from http://www.michaelleestallard.com/howard-schultzs-broken-heart

reduce violent crime and help victims: Serwer, A. (2004, January 26). Hot Starbucks to go. Fortune. Retrieved from http://archive.fortune.com/magazines/fortune/fortune_archive/2004/01/26/358850/index.htm

dissatisfied with their ethical climate: Covey, S. M. R., Link, G., & Merrill, R. R. (2012). Smart trust: Creating prosperity, energy, and joy in a low-trust world. New York: Free Press.

employee retention and job satisfaction: Egan, T. M., Yang, B., & Bartlett, K. R. (2004). The effects of organizational learning culture and job satisfaction on motivation to transfer learning and turnover intention. Human Resource Development Quarterly, 15(3), 279–301.

leads to organizational commitment: Mowday, R. T., Steers, R. M., & Porter, L. W. (1979). The measurement of organizational commitment. Journal of Vocational Behavior, 14(2), 224–247.

work engagement of employees: Yener, M., Yaldiran, M., & Ergun, S. (2012). The effect of ethical climate on work engagement. Procedia: Social and Behavioral Sciences, 58, 724–733.

same industry with low engagement: Gallup Research, 2009 report on employee engagement, spanning 152 global organizations.

ethical climate of companies and their employees: Stajkovic, A. D., & Luthans, F. (1997). Business ethics across cultures: A social cognitive model. Journal of World Business, 32(1), 17–34.

than formal ethics training: Adam, A. M., & Rachman-Moore, D. (2004). The methods used to implement an ethical code of conduct and employee attitudes. Journal of Business Ethics, 54(3), 225–244.

and increased profitability: McMurrian, R. C., & Matulich, E. (2006). Building customer value and profitability with business ethics. Journal of Business & Economics Research, 4(11), 11–18.

a better place to work: Donnelly, G. (2005, June 14). Beyond the code: Benchmarking ethics and compliance programs. Compliance Week. Retrieved from http://www.compliance-week.com/news/news-bulletin/beyond-the-code-benchmarking-ethics-and-compliance

and direct their decisions: Ibid.

apply the code of ethics on the job: Ibid.

has no effect at all: Ibid.

compared to those without codes: Fulmer, R. M. (2004). The challenge of ethical leadership. Organizational Dynamics, 33(3), 307–317.

had the biggest influence on them: Wiley, C. (2000). Ethical standards for human resource management professionals: A comparative analysis of five major codes. Journal of Business Ethics, 25(2), 93–114.

"what they're really saying is 'I value something else more.'": Smith, H. W. (2000). What matters most: The power of living your values. New York: Simon & Schuster.

studies carried out by the Institute for Global Ethics: Loges, W.E., Kidder, R.M. & Novak, C.R. (1999). Leadership and values: The people of Illinois and their community colleges. Camden, ME: Institute for Global Ethics, The Gallup Organization.

Chapter Two

tend to feel more alienated: Kasser, T., Ryan, R. M., Couchman, C. E., & Sheldon, K. M. (2004). Materialistic values: Their causes and consequences. In T. Kasser & A. D. Kanner (Eds.), Psychology and consumer culture: The struggle for a good life in a materialistic world (pp. 11–28). Washington, DC: American Psychological Association.

"still feel good about yourself.": Lynn, C. (2005). Avarice. Johns Hopkins Magazine, 57(4). Retrieved from http://www.jhu.edu/~jhumag/0905web/avarice1.html

believe they can get away with it: Nagin, D., Rebitzer, J. B., Sanders, S. G., & Taylor, L. J. (2002). Monitoring, motivation, and management: The determinants of opportunistic behavior in a field experiment. American Economic Review, 92(4), 850–873.

"lack of mutual confidence.": Arrow, K. J. (1972). Gifts and exchanges. Philosophy & Public Affairs, 1(4), 343–362.

"produce sustained innovation.": Friedman, T. L. (2005). The world is flat: A brief history of the twenty-first century. New York: Farrar, Straus and Giroux.

"trust reduces the cost of transactions.": Zak, P .J., & Knack, S. (2001). Trust and growth. Economic Journal, 111(470), 295–321.

"trusted brand is the most profitable.": Godin, S. (1999). Permission marketing: Turning strangers into friends, and friends into customers. New York: Simon & Schuster.

seriously violate the public trust: KPMG (2000). Organizational integrity survey.

ethical climate of society: Covey, Link, & Merrill (2012).

trust in senior management: Watson Wyatt survey, "Work USA 2004/2005."

than the previous year: Podolny, J. M. (2009). The buck stops (and starts) at business school. Harvard Business Review, 87(6), 62–67.

consistent with their actions: Maritz Research (2010). Managing in an era of distrust: Maritz Poll reveals employees lack trust in their workplace. Retrieved from http://www.maritz. com/Maritz-Poll/2010/Maritz-Poll-Reveals-Employees-Lack-Trust-in-their-Workplace.aspx

high-trust environment: Covey, S. R. (2004). The 8th habit: From effectiveness to greatness. New York: Free Press.

honesty and ethical standards: Gallup (2013). Honesty/ethics in professions. Retrieved from http://www.gallup.com/poll/1654/honesty-ethics-professions.aspx

good decisions in uncertain times: Maritz Research (2010).

accountable for results: Covey (2004).

with other departments: Ibid.

cares about their professional development: Age Wave and the Concours Group. (2005). New employer/employee equation survey.

cares about them in any way: Towers Perrin. (2003). The 2003 Towers Perrin talent report: Understanding what drives employee engagement.

improved problem solving: Cameron, K. S., Bright, D, & Caza, A. (2004). Exploring the relationships between OV and performance. American Behavioral Scientist, 47(6), 766–790. Kouzes, J. M., & Posner, B. Z. (2003). Encouraging the heart: A leader's guide to rewarding and recognizing others. San Francisco: Jossey-Bass. Covey (2004). Cameron, K. S., Dutton, J. E., & Quinn, R. E. (Eds.). (2003). Positive organizational scholarship: Foundations of a new discipline. San Francisco: Berrett-Koehler. Pfeffer, J. (1998). The human equation: Building profits by putting people first. Cambridge, MA: Harvard Business School Press.

higher levels of cooperation and greater employee perception of fairness: Burke, C. S., Sims, D. E., Lazzara, E. H., & Salas, E. (2007). Trust in leadership: A multi-level review and integration. Leadership Quarterly, 18(6), 606–632. Davis, J. H., Schoorman, F. D., Mayer, R. C., & Tan, H. H. (2000).

The trusted general manager and business unit performance: Empirical evidence of a competitive advantage. Strategic Management Journal, 21(5), 563–576. Dirks, K. T., & Skarlicki, D. (2004). Trust in leaders: Existing research and emerging issues. In R. M. Kramer & K. S. Cook (Eds.), Trust and distrust in organizations: Dilemmas and approaches (pp. 21–40). New York: Russell Sage Foundation. Zand, D. E. (1972). Trust and managerial problem solving. Administrative Science Quarterly, 17(2), 229–239. Hafer, C. L., & Olson, J. M. (2003). An analysis of empirical research on the scope of justice. Personality and Social Psychology Review, 7(4), 311–323.

success of a business: Fukuyama, F. (1995). Trust: The social virtues and the creation of prosperity. New York: Free Press.

both the job and leaders: Podsakoff, P. M., MacKenzie, S. B., Paine, J. B., & Bachrach, D. G. (2000). Organizational citizenship behavior: A critical review of the theoretical and empirical literature and suggestions for future research. Journal of Management, 26(3), 513–563. Konovsky, M. A., & Pugh, S. D. (1994). Citizenship behavior and social exchange. Academy of Management Journal, 37(3), 656–669. Dirks, K. T., & Ferrin, D. L. (2002). Trust in leadership: Meta-analytic findings and implications for research and practice. Journal of Applied Psychology, 87(4), 611–628.

the greater its economic strength: Akers, J. (1989). Ethics and competitiveness—putting first things first. Sloan Management Review, 30(2), 69–71.

high-trust companies than in low-trust companies: Covey, S. M. R. & Merrill, R. R. (2006). The speed of trust: The one thing that changes everything. New York: Free Press.

286 percent higher in high-trust companies: Watson Wyatt survey, "Work USA 2002."

outperformed the market by 288 percent: Ibid.

"what would the world be like?": Fryer, B. (2007). The ethical mind. Harvard Business Review, 85(3), 51–56.

"harm, offend, or treat unfairly.": Høgh-Olesen, H. (Ed.) (2010). Human morality and sociality: Evolutionary and comparative perspectives. Basingstoke, NY: Palgrave Macmillan.

"when it's absent, everybody notices.": Sandlund, C. (2002, October 1). Trust is a must. Entrepreneur. Retrieved from http://www.entrepreneur.com/article/55354

"any experience that reveals the human spirit.": Covey, Link, & Merrill (2012).

Chapter Three

average gain in productivity of 6 percent: Wagner, R., & Harter, J. K. (2006). 12: The elements of great managing. New York: Gallup Press.

known as an individual and treated as such: Cockerell, L. (2008). Creating magic: 10 common sense leadership strategies from a life at Disney. New York: Doubleday.

institutions where people work: Spears, L. C. (2004). Practicing servant-leadership. Leader to Leader, 2004(34), 7–11.

"I never learn a thing while I'm talking.": Thaler, L. K., & Koval, R. (2006). The power of nice: How to conquer the business world with kindness. New York: Doubleday.

Chapter Four

speed of the impact is over 250 miles per hour: Wald, M. L., & Baker, A. (2009, January 17). 1549 to tower: 'We're gonna end up in the Hudson.' New York Times. Retrieved from http://www.nytimes.com/2009/01/18/nyregion/18plane.html

"passengers brace for impact": Trotta, D. (2009, January 16). "New York hails pilot who landed jetliner on river." Reuters. Retrieved from http://www.reuters.com/article/2009/01/16/us-crash-newyork-idUSTRE50E8AI20090116

preparing for ditching the plane: National Transportation Safety Board (2010). Loss of thrust in both engines after encountering a flock of birds and subsequent ditching on the Hudson River, US Airways flight 1549, airbus A320-214, N106US, Weehawken, New Jersey, January 15, 2009. Aircraft accident report NTSB/AAR-10 /03. Washington, DC. Retrieved from http://www.ntsb.gov/doclib/reports/2010/AAR1003.pdf

study by Edison Research: Baer, J. (2014, September 28). 42 percent of consumers complaining in social media expect 60 minute response time. Convince & Convert. Retrieved from http://www.convinceandconvert.com/social-media-research/42-percent-of-consumers-complaining-in-social-media-expect-60-minute-response-time/

just over eleven hours: Conversocial. (2013). Twitter customer service report: July 2013: California retailers. Retrieved from http://landing.conversocial.com/hs-fs/hub/154001/file-235296003-pdf/California2013_July_Report.pdf

38 percent of customers: Lithium Technologies. (2013, October 29). Consumers will punish brands that fail to respond on

Twitter quickly. Lithium. Retrieved from http://www.lithium. com/company/news-room/press-releases/2013/consumers-will-punish-brands-that-fail-to-respond-on-twitter-quickly

20 to 40 percent more money with that company: Barry, C., Markey, R., Almquist, E. & Brahm, C. (2011, September 12). Putting social media to work. Bain & Company. Retrieved from   http://www.bain.com/publications/articles/putting-social-media-to-work.aspx

spring controls the electrical safety system: Jensen, C. (2014, March 2). In General Motors recalls, inaction and trail of fatal crashes. New York Times. Retrieved from http://www.nytimes. com/2014/03/03/business/in-general-motors-recalls-inaction-and-trail-of-fatal-crashes.html

8.5 million cars: Bennett, J. (2014, June 30). GM to recall 8.45 million more vehicles in North America. Wall Street Journal. Retrieved from http://online.wsj.com/articles/gm-to-recall-7-6-million-more-vehicles-in-u-s-1404153705

fined $35 million: Bennett, J., & White, J. B. (2014, May 16). GM gets record penalty for failing to report defect. Wall Street Journal. Retrieved from http://online.wsj.com/news/articles/SB10001424052702304908304579565692177164868

Ninety cents: Gara, T. (2014, April 1). GM ignition switch email. Scribd. Retrieved from: http://www.scribd.com/doc/215800826/GM-Ignition-Switch-Email

Chapter Five

96 percent report that they experience verbal abuse: Rowe, M. M., & Sherlock, H. (2005). Stress and verbal abuse in nursing: Do burned out nurses eat their young? Journal of Nursing Management, 13(3): 242–248.

Studies suggest: Cox, H. (1991). Verbal abuse nationwide, part II: Impact and modifications. Nursing Management, 22(3), 66–69. Oztunç, G. (2006). Examination of incidents of workplace verbal abuse against nurses. Journal of Nursing Care Quality, 21(4), 360–365. Roche, M., Diers, D., Duffield, C., & Catling-Paull, C. (2010). Violence toward nurses, the work environment, and patient outcomes. Journal of Nursing Scholarship, 42(1), 13–22.

"swearing at you and scolding you.": Kennedy, M., & Julie, H. (2013). Nurses' experiences and understanding of workplace violence in a trauma and emergency department in South Africa. Health SA Gesondheid, 18(1).

Seventy-two percent of nurses: Stone, T. E., & Hazelton, M. (2008). An overview of swearing and its impact on mental health nursing practice. International Journal of Mental Health Nursing, 17(3): 208–214.

do not report the incidents: Royal College of Nursing. (2002). Working well initiative: Dealing with bullying and harassment. London: Royal College of Nursing.

greater scrutiny or experience retaliation: Jones, J., & Lyneham, J. (2000). Violence: Part of the job for Australian nurses? Australian Journal of Advanced Nursing, 18(2), 27–32.

only 25 percent seek professional help: Zuzelo, P. R., Curran, S. S., & Zeserman, M. A. (2012). Registered nurses' and behavior health associates' responses to violent inpatient interactions on behavioral health units. Journal of the American Psychiatric Nurses Association 18(2), 112–126.

"and it is so unnecessary.": Kennedy & Julie (2013).

In 2012, CareerBuilder performed a survey: CareerBuilder. (2012, July 25). Swearing at work can harm your career prospects, finds CareerBuilder survey. CareerBuilder.com. Retrieved from http://www.careerbuilder.com/share/aboutus/pressreleasesdetail.aspx?sd=7%2f25%2f2012&siteid=cb-pr&sc_cmp1=cb_pr709_&id=pr709&ed=12%2f31%2f2012

"with less respect than one deserves.": Wolff, J. (1998). Fairness, respect, and the egalitarian ethos. Philosophy & Public Affairs, 27(2), 97–122.

"express myself in respectful terms.": Green, D., & Merrill, D. (2005). More than a hobby: How a $600 start-up became America's home & craft superstore. Nashville, TN: Thomas Nelson Publishers.

"appreciation and respect you have for your employees.": Cockerell (2008).

Chapter Six

exhibit openness, trust, and transparency: Gardner, W. L., Avolio, B. J., Luthans, F., May, D. R., & Walumbwa, F. (2005). "Can you see the real me?" A self-based model of authentic leader and follower development. Leadership Quarterly, 16(3), 343–372.

organizational and societal pressures: Peus, C., Wesche, J. S., Streicher, B., Braun, S., & Frey, D. (2012). Authentic leadership: An empirical test of its antecedents, consequences, and mediating mechanisms. Journal of Business Ethics, 107(3), 331–348.

"biblical definition of the family unit.": Blume, K. A. (2012, July 16). 'Guilty as charged,' Cathy says of Chick-fil-A's stand on biblical & family values. Baptist Press. Retreived from http://www.bpnews.net/38271

12 percent increase in sales in 2012: Satran, J. (2013, January 31). Chick-fil-A sales soar in 2012 despite bad PR. Huffington Post. Retrieved from http://www.huffingtonpost.com/2013/01/31/chick-fil-a-sales-2012_n_2590612.html

Shane wrote an article in the Huffington Post: Windmeyer, S. L. (2013, January 28). Dan and me: My coming out as a friend of Dan Cathy and Chick-fil-A. Huffington Post. Retrieved from http://www.huffingtonpost.com/shane-l-windmeyer/dan-cathy-chick-fil-a_b_2564379.html

Chapter Seven

Negative effects include: Boggs, L., Carr, S. C., Fletcher, R. B., & Clarke, D. E. (2005). Pseudoparticipation in communication networks: The social psychology of broken promises. Journal of Social Psychology, 145(5), 621–624. Buyukyilmaz, O., & Cakmak, A. F. (2013). Direct and indirect effects of psychological contract breach on academicians' turnover intention in Turkey. Journal of Business, Economics & Finance, 2(4), 50–66. Kickul, J. (2001). Promises made, promises broken: An exploration of employee attraction and retention practices in small business. Journal of Small Business Management, 39(4), 320–335.

Chapter Eight

evidenced by a 1998 study in the workplace: Verizon Conferencing. (1998). Meetings in America: A study of trends, costs and attitudes toward business travel, teleconferencing, and their impact on productivity. Greenwich, CT: INFOCOMM.

Chapter Nine

In 52 years: WFAA Staff (2013, November 8). Arlington police report details woman's death after fall from Texas Giant. WFAA. Retrieved from http://www.wfaa.com/story/news/local/tarrant-county/2014/08/19/14125134/

shy away from adventure: Shoichet, C.E. (2013, July 22). Roller coaster ride became 'nightmare' for Texas woman's family. CNN. Retrieved from http://www.cnn.com/2013/07/21/us/texas-roller-coaster-death/

"As long as you heard it click": Ibid.

daughter and son-in-law: WFAA Staff (2013, November 8). Arlington police report details woman's death after fall from Texas Giant.

after a fourteen-story ascent: WFAA Staff (2013, July 20). Family identifies woman killed on Six Flags ride. WFAA. Retrieved from http://www.wfaa.com/story/news/local/2014/08/19/14070830/

a loud pop: WFAA Staff (2013, November 8). Pictures captured the moments immediately following death on Six Flags ride. WFAA. Retrieved from http://www.wfaa.com/story/news/local/tarrant-county/2014/08/19/14125534/

"She fell!": WFAA Staff (2013, July).

"We need to go get her!": Eiserer, T. (2013, July 20). Family identifies Dallas resident who was victim of Texas Giant accident. Dallas News. Retrieved from http://www.dallasnews.

com/news/metro/20130719-breaking-news-arlington-police-fire-at-six-flags-for-fatal-incident-texas-giant-said-to-be-involved.ece

"We are deeply saddened": WFAA Staff (2013, July). statement on the date of the reopening: WFAA Staff (2013, November 8). Arlington police report details woman's death after fall from Texas Giant.

Chapter Ten

Her throat hurts and she sniffles: Bell, R. The Tylenol terrorist. Crime Library. Retrieved from http://www.crimelibrary.com/terrorists_spies/terrorists/tylenol_murders/index.html

"Mary, are you okay?": Chicago. (2012, September 21). Chicago Tylenol murders: An oral history. Chicagomag.com. Retrieved from http://www.chicagomag.com/Chicago-Magazine/October-2012/Chicago-Tylenol-Murders-An-Oral-History/

hears her mother's strenuous breathing: Babwin, D. (2007, September 29). Tylenol tampering case remains unsolved, in 25 years. USA Today. Retrieved from http://usatoday30.usatoday.com/news/health/2007-09-29-tylenol-poisonings_N.htm

"this is the first we are hearing of this": U. S. Department of Defense. Case study: The Johnson & Johnson Tylenol crisis. Crisis Communication Strategies. Retrieved from http://www.ou.edu/deptcomm/dodjcc/groups/02C2/Johnson%20&%20Johnson.htm

"We've got to recall it.": Josephson, M. (2012, October 7). The legacy of Johnson & Johnson and James Burke—an extraordinary leader. Josephson Institute. Retrieved from http://

josephsoninstitute.org/business/blog/2012/10/the-legacy-of-johnson-johnson-and-james-burke-an-extraordinary-leader/

"can bring a major corporation to its knees.": Notredame-business. (2011, November 18). Tylenol crisis [Online video]. Retrieved from https://www.youtube.com/watch?v=zPccWP-CF9Ak

"protecting the people.": U. S. Department of Defense.

"toll-free customer support hotlines": Josephson (2012).

seven people were assembled: U. S. Department of Defense.

seven total deaths: Chicago (2012).

immediately stop using Tylenol: U. S. Department of Defense.

more than 450,000 doctors' offices and hospitals: Josephson (2012).

cost the company $100 million: Ibid.

world's first tamper-resistant bottle: Susi, R. (2002). The Tylenol crisis, 1982. Effective Crisis Management. Retrieved from http://iml.jou.ufl.edu/projects/fall02/susi/tylenol.htm

2,250 presentations: Ibid.

regained 70 percent of its market share: Baker, M. Johnson & Johnson and Tylenol. MallenBaker.net. Retrieved from http://www.mallenbaker.net/csr/crisis02.php

A part of the company's Code of Ethics: Johnson & Johnson. Ethical code for the conduct of pharmaceutical medicine.

Investor.jnj.com. Retrieved from http://www.investor.jnj.com/ethics.cfm

His leadership earned him: Josephson (2012).

He died on September 28: Ibid.

humility, fairness, and utilitarian qualities: Collins, J. (2001). Good to Great. New York: Harper-Collins.

good apologies have four key elements: Friedman, H. H., Lopez-Pumarejo, T., & Friedman, L. W. (2006). The largest minority group: The disabled. Business Quest. Retrieved from http://www.westga.edu/~bquest/2006/disabled.pdf

is low and continues to decline: Ferrin, D. L., Kim, P. H., Cooper, C. D., & Dirks, K. T. (2007). Silence speaks volumes: The effectiveness of reticence in comparison to apology and denial for responding to integrity- and competence-based trust violations. Journal of Applied Psychology, 9(4), 893–908.

"carved out of the warped wood of humanity.": Ciulla, J. B. (2001). Carving leaders from the warped wood of humanity. Canadian Journal of Administrative Sciences, 18(4), 313–319.

findings of multiple studies have revealed: Barkan, R., Ayal, S., Gino, F., & Ariely, D. (2012). The pot calling the kettle black: Distancing response to ethical dissonance. Journal of Experimental Psychology, 141(4), 757–773.

The moral hypocrisy of company leadership: Falk, C. F., & Blaylock, B. K. (2012). The H factor: A behavioral explanation of leadership failures in the 2007–2009 financial system meltdown. Journal of Leadership, Accountability & Ethics, 9(2), 68–82.

Chapter Eleven

Jim Kouzes and Barry Posner, found in their studies: Kouzes, J. M., & Posner, B. Z. (1992). Ethical leaders: An essay about being in love. Journal of Business Ethics, 11(5/6), 479–484.

110.8 million viewers: Gallo, P. (2013, February 4). Beyonce's Super Bowl halftime draws estimated 104 million viewers. Billboard. Retrieved from http://www.billboard.com/biz/articles/news/tv-film/1537723/beyonces-super-bowl-halftime-show-draws-estimated-104-million

268,000 tweets per minute: Hu, E. (2013, August 12). The biggest Twitter moments ever feature Beyonce, Romney. NPR. Retrieved from http://www.npr.org/blogs/alltechconsidered/2013/08/12/211410644/the-biggest-twitter-moments-ever-feature-beyonce-romney

"part tutorial on how to dazzle an audience.": Newman, M. (2013, February 3). Review: Beyonce delivers a sexy, if rushed, Super Bowl half-time show. HitFix. Retrieved from http://www.hitfix.com/news/review-beyonce-delivers-a-sexy-if-rushed-super-bowl-half-time-show

"Now that was a halftime show": Sheffield, R. (2013, February 4). Super Bowl XLVII: The night belonged to Beyonce. Rolling Stone. Retrieved from http://www.rollingstone.com/music/news/super-bowl-xlvii-the-night-belonged-to-beyonce-20130204

In 2003, three executives of CIBC: Schwartz, M. S. (2013). Developing and sustaining an ethical corporate culture: The core elements. Business Horizons, 56(1), 39–50.

In 2002, Starwood Hotels did a study: Hotel Online. (2002, June 26). Starwood Hotels study finds 43% of execs say some of their biggest deals have been done on the golf course; and not surprising—82% admit to cheating on the golf course. Hotel-online.com. Retrieved from http://hotel-online.com/News/PR2002_2nd/Jun02_HOTGolf.html

Chapter Twelve

number one cause of preventable tragic events: Stimmel, M. (2009). Disruptive behavior and miscommunication in health care settings. Senior Honors Theses, Paper 234. Retrieved from http://commons.emich.edu/honors/234

about 25 percent efficiency: Husman, R. C., Lahiff, J. M., & Penrose, J. M. (1988). Business communication: Strategies and skills. Chicago: Dryden Press.

Chapter Thirteen

tools in an adult bully's arsenal: Sutton, R. (2007). Building the civilized workplace. McKinsey Quarterly, 2, 47–55.

48 percent of employees: Yüksel, M. (2010). Mobbing: Psychological terrorism at workplace. In B. B. Hawks & L. Baruh (Eds.), Conference proceedings of the International Conference on Conflict, Terrorism and Society: Societies under siege: Media, government, politics, and citizens' freedoms in an age of terrorism (pp. 138–147). Istanbul: Kadir Has University.

"like Chinese water torture.": Tracy, S. J., Lutgen-Sandvik, P., & Alberts, J. K. (2006). Nightmares, demons, and slaves: Exploring the painful metaphors of workplace bullying. Management Communication Quarterly, 20(2), 148–185.

Studies have revealed that tactics: Ibid.

51 percent higher rate of absenteeism: Kivimäki, M., Elovainio, M., & Vahtera, J. (2000). Workplace bullying and sickness absence in hospital staff. Occupational and Environmental Medicine, 57(10), 656–660.

45 percent higher rate of stress-related health problems: Workplace Bullying Institute and Zogby International. (2007). U.S. workplace bullying survey. Retrieved from http://workplacebullying.org/multi/pdf/WBIsurvey2007.pdf

25 percent resignation rate because of bullying: Daniel, T. A. (2006). Bullies in the workplace: A focus on the "abusive disrespect" of employees [White paper]. Retrieved from http://www.noworkplacebullies.com/assets/docs/BulliesintheWorkplace1_HR_Magazine.234101040.pdf

89 percent of respondents in one survey: Lindenberger, J. (2012). The bullies have left the playground. Lindenberger Group. Retreived from http://www.lindenbergergroup.com/the_bully.html

The negative impacts of bullying that companies experience: DiFonzo, N., & Bordia, P. (2000). How top PR professionals handle hearsay: Corporate rumors, their effects, and strategies to manage them. Public Relations Review, 26(2), 173–190.

37 percent of the entire U.S. workforce: Workplace Bullying Institute and Zogby International (2007).

In 2001, Lars Dalgaard created SuccessFactors: Sutton (2007).

"People are hired and fired for attitude": Cohen, A., Watkinson, J., & Boone, J. (2005, March 28). Southwest Airlines

CEO grounded in real world. SearchCIO. Retrieved from http://searchcio.techtarget.com/news/1071837/Southwest-Airlines-CEO-grounded-in-real-world

Chapter Fourteen

"the feeling you are participating in a crusade.": Mackey, J., & Sisodia, R. (2013). Conscious capitalism: Liberating the heroic spirit of business. Boston: Harvard Business Review Press.

Memorial Day 1981: Ibid

Zaz Lamarr's mother was becoming more ill: Jaffe, J. (2010). Flip the funnel: How to use existing customers to gain new ones. Hoboken, N.J: Wiley.

"I Heart Zappos": Marco, M. (2007, October 16). Zappos sends you flowers. Consumerist. Retrieved from http://consumerist.com/2007/10/16/zappos-sends-you-flowers/

than companies in the highest 25 percent: Harter, J. K., Schmidt, F. L., Killham, E. A., & Asplund, J. W. (2006). Q12 meta-analysis. Omaha, NE: Gallup Organization.

Another study finds that ethical companies: Ferrell, O. C. (2004). Business ethics and customer satisfaction. Academy of Management Executives, 18(2), 126–129.

equates to a 1 percent increase in revenues: Goleman, D., Boyatzis, R., & McKee, A. (2002). Primal leadership: Realizing the power of emotional intelligence. Boston: Harvard Business School Press.

Chapter Fifteen

"We need new leadership": George, B. (2003). Authentic leadership: Rediscovering the secrets to creating lasting value. San Francisco: Jossey-Bass.

Paul O'Neill understands this: Schwartz (2013).

graduates from Carnegie Mellon: Cable, J. (2013, October 3). NSC 2013: O'Neill exemplifies safety leadership. EHS Today. Retrieved from http://ehstoday.com/safety/nsc-2013-oneill-exemplifies-safety-leadership

His philosophy on safety: Roth, M. (2012, May 13). 'Habitual excellence': The workplace according to Paul O'Neill. Pittsburgh Post-Gazette. Retrieved from http://www.post-gazette.com/business/businessnews/2012/05/13/Habitual-excellence-The-workplace-according-to-Paul-O-Neill/stories/201205130249

from 1.86 lost workdays per 100 workers to 0.2: Ibid.

"Empathetic people are superb at": Goleman, Boyatzis, & McKee (2002).

Gallup's poll of more than two million employees: Ibid.

One study found that work environments: Resick, C. J., Baltes, B. B., & Shantz, C. W. (2007). Person-organization fit and work-related attitudes and decisions: Examining interactive effects with job fit and conscientiousness. Journal of Applied Psychology, 92(5), 1446–55.

Chapter Sixteen

The flight attendant's name is Yvonne LeMaster: Suskind, R. (2003, January 13). Humor has returned to Southwest Airlines. Wall Street Journal. Retrieved from http://online.wsj.com/news/articles/SB1042409678722754624

part of the company's core values: Southwest Airlines. Culture: Values. Southwest.com. Retrieved from http://www.southwest.com/html/about-southwest/careers/culture.html

It is a part of the company's recruitment process: Suskind (2003).

"There are only two emotions on a plane": (1985, May 6). Orson Welles, interview to celebrate his 70th birthday. Times of London.

This is no industry secret either: Southwest Airlines. Southwest corporate fact sheet. Swamedia.com. Retrieved from http://www.swamedia.com/channels/Corporate-Fact-Sheet/pages/corporate-fact-sheet

He reports findings showing that jokes and laughter: Goleman, Boyatzis, & McKee (2002).

three times the number of witty remarks: Ibid.

quicker than irritability and gloominess: Thaler & Koval (2006).

Other studies show that smiles: Myers, D. G. (2000). Feeling good about Fredrickson's positive emotions. Prevention & Treatment 3(1).

It has led the company to total operating revenues: Southwest Airlines. Southwest Corporate Fact Sheet. SWAmedia. com. Retrieved from http://www.swamedia.com/channels/ Corporate-Fact-Sheet/pages/corporate-fact-sheet

2014 Best Companies for Leaders: Southwest Airlines. Southwest Corporate Fact Sheet. SWAmedia.com. Retrieved from http://www.swamedia.com/channels/Corporate-Fact-Sheet/ pages/corporate-fact-sheet

Chapter Seventeen

One study shows that organizations: de Waal, A. A. (2012). Characteristics of high performance organisations. Business Management and Strategy, 3(1), 28–45.

Epilogue

one of the largest corporate bankruptcies in history: Benston, G. J. (2003, November 6). Policy Analysis: The quality of corporate financial statements and their auditors before and after Enron. Washington DC: Cato Institute. Retrieved from http://www.cato.org/sites/cato.org/ files/pubs/pdf/pa497.pdf

Acknowledgements

To Matthew Kelly for your counsel, your publishing expertise, your brilliant team, and your own daily example that living with strong values can and does inspire all around us.

To Jordan Ochel for your gift with the written word and for all the hours you put in on weekends and late nights after your day job. Your tireless work to research the content for this book and to assist me with my message are proof that nothing equals the power of great story-telling.

To Brian Tracy for writing a beautiful foreword to this book and underscoring the importance of the message for *Values, Inc.* Your association with this work speaks volumes, and I am honored to include you.

To the entire Dwyer Group team led by Chief Executive Officer Mike Bidwell, Executive Vice President Mary Thompson, Executive Vice President Robert Tunmire, Chief Financial Officer Tom Buckley, Chief Administrative Officer Debbie Hood, and General Counsel Duke Johnston who strive to live R.I.C.H. and make this story possible.

To Kym Surridge and Tom Buckley for a masterful job of proof-reading this work, so that all may enjoy.

To Carol Dugat and Julie Potts for your unwavering assistance to keep me organized, focused, and on time.

To BizCom Associates and my publicist Monica Feid, for helping with this project and the promotion of this book.

To the many individuals who allowed us to share their stories in this book – Béla Szigethy, Stewart Kohl, Sam Katz, Russ Stacey, Brandon Haire, Larry Ross, Mike Morales, Patrick Smith, Ken Henriksen, Sam Stevens Jr., and Doug Baker

And to the wonderful friends and colleagues who have endorsed *Values, Inc.* including:

Ken Blanchard	Joe Polish
Matthew Kelly	Gregory W. Slayton
Dr. Ben Carson	Lisa Huetteman
Chris Carlson	Barbara Glanz
Sharon Lechter	Béla Szigethy
John Assaraf	Greg Reid
Verne Harnish	Sam Katz
Stewart Kohl	Robert Cooper
Shep Hyken	Margaret McEntire
Eric Chester	Walter Bond
Tommy Spaulding	Cathy Lee Crosby
	Steve Caldeira

About the Author

Dina Dwyer-Owens

Dina Dwyer-Owens serves as Co-Chair of The Dwyer Group®, a parent company whose concepts include more than 1,700 franchises across the world operating under the service brands of Aire Serv®, Glass Doctor®, Mr. Appliance®, Mr. Electric®, Mr. Rooter® (Drain Doctor® in the U.K. and Portugal), Rainbow International®, The Grounds Guys® and Five Star Painting®. Collectively, The Dwyer Group service brands account for almost $1 billion in annual systemwide sales. Dina's duties include cultivating the R.I.C.H. corporate culture, high level strategic planning, acquisitions and public relations. She served as the 2010 Chairwoman for the International Franchise Association and is also responsible for reintroducing the IFA's VetFran program, where participating franchisors offer their best financial incentives to military veterans who want to own a franchise. She has been honored throughout her career with numerous awards including the 2012 Ernst & Young Entrepreneur of the Year Award for the Southwest Area North, the 2012 Small Business Influencer Award, and the national Raising a Ruckus Award from Working Mother magazine. In 2012, she appeared on "Undercover Boss" and in 2013 she appeared on the first-ever "Undercover Boss: Epic Bosses" episode, sharing with millions of viewers her faith, her passion for business and her belief in The Dwyer Group Code of Values.

Under her leadership, *The Dwyer Group* has grown and received many honors including having *The Dwyer Group* brands listed among Entrepreneur magazine's "Franchise 500" list of best franchise companies for several years running.

We Serve. You Save.

We've helped more than one thousand entrepreneurs start their own business.

Will You Be Next?

Leading the service industry is more than a statement at The Dwyer Group®. It means providing the best experience for our customers and franchise owners without compromise.

It's about reaching financial and personal goals while maintaining a commitment to integrity. It's about creating businesses that communities can look to for more than just service.

Our family of companies has more than 90 years of combined experience in helping entrepreneurs reach their goal of business ownership. And we can help you too.

855-582-9785
www.LeadingTheServiceIndustry.com

Share *Values, Inc.* with everyone you know!

Whether you just want another copy or you want a hundred copies for colleagues and clients, visit

Values-Inc.com

for great bulk purchasing opportunities!